This
BIBLE STORY BOOK

is presented

to _Jenny and Jamie_

by _Aunt Marion_

for _happy reading_

date _August 1987_

My Family Tree

My Name _____

Date of Birth _____

Place of Birth _____

Brother _____

Date of Birth _____

Place of Birth _____

Sister _____

Date of Birth _____

Place of Birth _____

Brother _____

Date of Birth _____

Place of Birth _____

Sister _____

Date of Birth _____

Place of Birth _____

Mother's Name _____

Date of Birth _____

Place of Birth _____

_____   _____

Brother   Sister

_____   _____

Date of Birth   Date of Birth

_____   _____
Brother   Sister

_____   _____
Date of Birth   Date of Birth

_____   _____
Maternal Grandfather   Maternal Grandmother

_____   _____
Date of Birth   Date of Birth

_____   _____
Place of Birth   Place of Birth

⌒∽◦∼⌒

Father's Name_____

Date of Birth_____

Place of Birth_____

_____   _____
Brother   Sister

_____   _____
Date of Birth   Date of Birth

_____   _____
Brother   Sister

_____   _____
Date of Birth   Date of Birth

_____   _____
Paternal Grandfather   Paternal Grandmother

_____   _____
Date of Birth   Date of Birth

_____   _____
Place of Birth   Place of Birth

Memories

My church is _____

_____

My pastor is _____

My Sunday school teachers:

    Name _____ Year _____

    Name _____ Year _____

    Name _____ Year _____

My favorite Bible story is _____

My favorite Bible character is _____

My favorite Bible verse is _____

_____

My best friends in Christ are:

    Name _____ Age _____

    Name _____ Age _____

    Name _____ Age _____

Special Events in My Christian Life

_____

_____

_____

_____

_____

Bible Story Book
NEW TESTAMENT

Bible Story Book
NEW TESTAMENT

Sarah Fletcher

Illustrated by Edward Ostendorf

Publishing House
St. Louis

Cover illustration by Don Kueker

Library of Congress Cataloging in Publication Data

    Bible story book, New Testament.

    Summary: sixty-three New Testament stories presented in
chronological order, with a Bible reference and contemporary prayer
at the conclusion of each.
    1. Bible stories, English—N.T. [1. Bible stories—N.T.] I. Title.
BS2400.G73 1983   225.9'505   83-1813
ISBN 0-570-04080-9

1 2 3 4 5 6 7 8 9 10 PP 92 91 90 89 88 87 86 85 84 83

Contents

The Birth of John

When Herod was king of Judea, there lived a priest called Zechariah and his wife Elizabeth. They were good people and served God faithfully. But they were growing old and still had no children.

One day Zechariah was in the Holy Place of the temple, burning incense at a small gold-covered altar. Everyone else was outside praying. All at once an angel appeared and stood on the right side of the altar. Zechariah was terrified.

"Don't be afraid, Zechariah," said the angel. "God has heard your prayer. Elizabeth will have a son and you must call him John. Many people will rejoice because he is born, and he will be great in God's sight. He will be filled with the Holy Spirit and will bring many people back to God. He will go before the Lord and make the people ready for Him."

"How can I be sure of this?" asked Zechariah. "I'm an old man and Elizabeth isn't so young either."

"I am Gabriel," said the angel. "I stand in God's presence and have been sent to bring you this good news. But since you haven't believed me, you won't be able to speak until all these things happen."

Meanwhile, the people outside were waiting for Zechariah. When he finally came out of the Holy Place, he couldn't say a word. He could only make signs. Then the people knew he had seen a vision.

Zechariah went home, and soon after, Elizabeth discovered she was going to have a baby.

"God has done this for me," she said, and she was very happy.

Finally the child was born, a little boy, and all of Elizabeth's relatives and neighbors rejoiced with her.

After eight days it was time to name the child. All the friends and relatives thought Elizabeth would call him Zechariah, after his father. But Elizabeth shook her head.

"He is to be called John," she said.

"No one in your family is called that," said the people. They made signs to Zechariah to find out what he wanted to call the baby. Zechariah asked for a writing tablet.

"His name is John," he wrote. And at that moment Zechariah was able to speak again. At once he praised God.

All the neighbors were surprised and couldn't stop talking about what had happened.

"What will this child grow up to be?" they wondered.

Then Zechariah was filled with the Holy Spirit and said:

"Blessed be the Lord our God, for He has come to us. He has given us a way of salvation, just as He promised. He saved our ancestors from their enemies, and He still remembers His holy covenant. He will save us too and set us free to serve Him all our life.

"And you, little child, shall be called Prophet of the Most High, because you will go before the Lord to prepare the way for Him. You will tell His people about salvation through the forgiveness of their sins. You will tell them about God's mercy and how He is bringing light to those who live in darkness and the shadow of death, light that will lead our feet in the way of peace."

Years passed and little John grew up. He lived in the wilderness until it was time for him to appear before the people of Israel. ∎

Luke 1:5-25, 57-80

Prayer

If I saw an angel, Father,
I think I'd scream.
And if he told me something
like he told Zechariah, well,
I don't know what I'd do.
I might not believe him either.
At first I thought the angel
was punishing Zechariah
by not letting him speak.
But now I don't think so.
I think he was giving Zechariah a chance
to stop all that talking and just think,
to understand that this was You, Father,
who was interrupting his life for a very
good reason.
Zechariah finally did understand, too, Father,
that You were going to do things Your way
and he was glad.
Father, You're in charge of my life.
Whatever You have in mind for me, well,
I'm glad!

Amen.

An Angel Comes to Mary

About six months after the angel Gabriel talked to Zechariah, God sent him to a town in Galilee called Nazareth. There lived a young girl called Mary, and she was engaged to be married to a man called Joseph.

"Rejoice, favored one!" said Gabriel to Mary. "The Lord is with you."

Mary didn't know what this meant, and she was upset.

"Don't be afraid, Mary," said Gabriel. "You have found favor with God. You are going to have a Son and you must call Him Jesus. He will be great and He will be called Son of the Most High. God will give Him the throne of His ancestor, David, and He will rule forever and ever."

"But how can this happen?" asked Mary. "I am not married."

"God's Spirit will come to you," said Gabriel, "and your Child will be called the Son of God. Your relative Elizabeth is also going to have a son, even though she is old. You see, nothing is impossible for God."

"I am God's servant," said Mary. "Whatever He wants to happen, let it be."

After the angel left her, Mary set off for the town in the hills of Judea where Elizabeth and Zechariah lived. She went into their house and called out a greeting. As soon as Elizabeth heard the greeting, the child inside her leaped, and Elizabeth was filled with the Holy Spirit.

"You are the most blessed of women," she said to Mary, "and the Child you are carrying is blessed. Why should I be honored by a visit from the mother of my Lord? Oh, you are blessed, Mary, because you have believed that the promise God made to you would be kept!"

Then Mary sang a magnificent song: "My soul says that the Lord is great and my spirit is glad because of my Savior. He has paid attention to me, His lowly servant.

From now on everyone will call me blessed, because God has done great things for me. Holy is His name and His mercy reaches from age to age. He has shown His power and upset the proud in heart. He has pulled princes off their thrones and lifted up lowly people. He has filled the hungry with good things, but He has sent the rich away empty. Because of His mercy, He has come to help His servant, Israel, just as He promised our ancestors."

Mary stayed with Elizabeth for three months. Then she went home again. ■

Luke 1:26-56

Prayer

I know just how she felt, Father!
When Mary went to see her cousin
and sang that song of praise
—I've felt like that.
You've done great things for me too.
Sometimes I've felt like a nothing.
I couldn't think of one reason
why I should be alive.
I didn't think anyone liked me
and I didn't like myself very much.
I wanted to crawl into a hole
and never come out.
But You pulled me away from that hole.
You picked me up and dusted me off.
You helped me stand again, strong and sure.
You announced loud and clear
that I am Yours.
Oh, Father, how great You are!

Amen.

Jesus Is Born

Joseph didn't know what to do when he found out that Mary was going to have a baby. He knew that he wasn't the father, and he thought he should probably break his engagement with Mary. But he decided to do this very privately, so Mary wouldn't be disgraced.

Then one night God sent an angel to Joseph in a dream.

"Joseph, son of David," said the angel, "don't be afraid to marry Mary. The Child she is going to have is God's Son. You must call Him Jesus because He is the one who will save His people from sin."

When Joseph woke up, he did what the angel said and married Mary. It would have been nice then if the two of them could have settled down in a little house in Nazareth and waited for Jesus to be born. But that's not how things worked.

Instead the Roman emperor, Caesar Augustus, sent out a command that everyone in the land had to be counted. Furthermore, they had to be counted in the town their ancestors came from. This meant that Joseph had to go to Bethlehem because it was the town David came from, and David was Joseph's ancestor. Mary had to go with him and be counted too, so together they made the long, hard trip.

When they got to Bethlehem, the town was overflowing with other people who had come to be counted too. Mary and Joseph couldn't find anyplace to stay. Finally the person who ran the inn said that they could stay in the stable.

So Mary and Joseph stumbled to the stable and there little Jesus was born. Mary wrapped Him in swaddling clothes and laid him in a manger, a long, narrow box that cows and donkeys ate from. You see, there weren't any cradles in a stable.

Just outside town were some fields where shepherds kept their sheep. The shepherds didn't know anything special had happened. They were just doing their job and looking after their sheep as usual.

Then, all at once, God's angel appeared to them, and God's glory shone like a great light all around them. The shepherds were scared to death.

"Don't be afraid," said the angel. "I bring you good news, news of great joy that will be shared with all people. Today in David's town a Savior has been born, and He is Christ, the Lord. And here is how you can be sure. You will find a Baby who is wrapped in swaddling clothes and lying in a manger."

Then a great crowd of angels appeared, all praising God and saying: "Glory to God in the highest and peace on earth to all whom He loves."

Of course, the shepherds were terribly excited, and as soon as the angels had gone, they began saying to one another, "Let's go down to Bethlehem and see this thing that the angels told us about!"

So they hurried into the town and found Mary and Joseph and the Baby, who was lying in a manger. They told Mary and Joseph what the angel had said, and they told a lot of other people too. It was such good news that they just couldn't keep it to themselves. Finally, though, they went back to their fields, praising God for everything that had happened.

And Mary remembered all these things and thought and thought about them. ∎

Matthew 1:18-25;
Luke 2:1-20

Prayer

Gloria! Gloria! Gloria!
Oh, Father, how I wish
I could have heard those words
roll out in great angel voices.
How I wish I could have run
under star-hung skies with the shepherds
down to Bethlehem.
How I wish I could have stood
knee-deep in the crackling straw
and looked by the light of a lantern
at Him.
I am here in another country, another time.
And yet,
I hear,
I run,
I look,
in my heart, Father,
every year.
Gloria! Gloria! Gloria!

Amen.

At the Temple

After eight days, it was time for Mary and Jospeh to officially name their baby. Of course they called Him Jesus, as the angel had said they should.

In the Law that Moses gave the people, it also said that firstborn baby boys should be brought before the Lord and promised as a servant to God. At the same time, two pigeons should be sacrificed. So, 40 days after Jesus was born Mary and Joseph went to the temple in Jerusalem and did this too.

Now at that time there was an old man called Simeon living in Jerusalem. He was a good man and believed that one day God would send a Savior. In fact, God's Spirit had told Simeon that he would not die until he had seen the Savior God had promised to send.

God's Spirit told Simeon to go to the temple the same day Mary and Joseph went there with Jesus. As soon as he saw the Baby, Simeon took Him into his arms and blessed God.

"Now, Lord, You can let Your servant go in peace," he said, "just as You promised. For I have seen the Savior whom You have sent for all nations. He will be a light to shine on the people who do not know You, and He will be the glory of Your people, Israel."

Mary and Joseph just stood there, wondering what all of this meant. Then Simeon blessed them too and spoke to Mary.

"This Child will cause many people to fall in Israel," he said, "and many to stand up. People will turn away from Him and you will suffer. But because of Him, many secrets will be told."

In the temple was also a woman called Anna. She was 84 years old, and she stayed there all the time, serving God and praying. Anna came by just as Simeon was talking to Mary. At once she began to praise God.

And from then on, whenever Anna met people who were still waiting for God to keep His promise and send a Savior, she told them about Jesus. ■

Luke 2:22-40

Prayer

Simeon saw and his tired old eyes
must have been filled with light.
He had heard Your promise, Father.
He knew You were a Promise-Maker.
But then he saw the Child, Your Son,
and knew You were a Promise-Keeper.
I have seen Him too, that Child.
I have seen Him in Your church
and in the words of your Holy Book.
I have seen Him in my heart
and in the hearts of others.
I know too that You are a Promise-Keeper
and the light of that Promise
fills my life.

Amen.

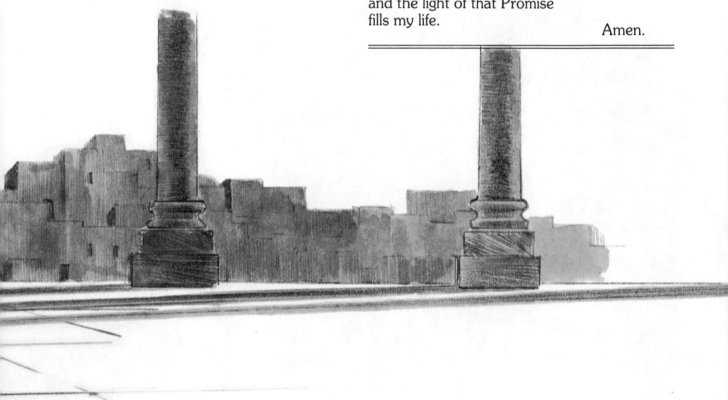

The Wise Men and the Flight

After Jesus had been born, some Wise Men came to Jerusalem from their home in the East.

"Where is the Baby King of the Jews?" they asked. "We saw His star, and we have come to worship Him."

Someone told King Herod what the Wise Men had said, and he became terribly upset. He didn't like the idea of another king in his country. So he called together all the religious leaders and asked them where God was supposed to send the Savior.

"He will be born in Bethlehem," said the leaders. "A long time ago a prophet wrote that the ruler of God's people would be born there, even though it is a little town."

Then Herod sent for the Wise Men.

"Tell me about this star," he said. "On what day did you first see it?"

They told him, and Herod said they should travel on to Bethlehem.

"Come back this way, though," he added, "and tell me all about the Child. I want to know exactly where He is; so I can go and worship Him too."

The Wise Men left the palace and set out for Bethlehem. The star they had seen went before them and led them right to the house where Mary and Joseph were living with little Jesus. They went inside, and as soon as they saw Jesus with His mother, they fell down on

their knees and worshiped Him. Then they opened their packs and gave Him presents of gold, frankincense, and myrrh.

That night the Wise Men had a dream, and in the dream God warned them not to go back to Jerusalem and see King Herod. So they went home a different way.

After they had gone, God sent an angel to Joseph in a dream.

"Get up," said the angel. "Take the Child and His mother and run away to Egypt. Stay there until I tell you, because Herod is planning to find the Child and kill Him."

Joseph got up at once, and that very night he and Mary took little Jesus and ran away to Egypt.

Meanwhile, Herod was furious when he found out that the Wise Men weren't coming back to him. He ordered his soldiers to kill all the little boys in Bethlehem and the area around it who were two years old or younger. He thought he'd be sure to get Jesus that way.

But Jesus was safe with His parents in Egypt, and they stayed there until King Herod died. Then an angel came to Jospeh again in a dream.

"Get up, Joseph," said the angel. "The three of you can go back to the land of Israel now because Herod is dead."

So Joseph got up and took his family back to Israel. They didn't go to Bethlehem, though, because Herod's son was king, and he wasn't very nice either. Instead they went back to the town of Nazareth. ■

Matthew 2

Prayer

It's amazing, Father!
He was only a little boy
and already someone wanted to kill Him!
How can people be like that?
How can they care so much about themselves
that they completely turn away from You
and even try to kill Your Son?
Is it greed
that makes them be that way?
Do things like crowns and power
—and money, I guess—
become so important to them
that there's no room for anything else
in their lives?
I'd hate that, Father.
Please don't ever let me become that greedy.
Please let me always have room in my life for You.
Why, You're what life is all about!

Amen.

Jesus and the Teachers

Every year Mary and Joseph traveled to Jerusalem for the Passover, that great feast the people of Israel had celebrated ever since God led them out of slavery in Egypt. When Jesus was 12 years old, Mary and Joseph went to the feast as usual and took Him with them.

In those days people used to travel together whenever they could. It was safer for them to be with a bunch of other people. That way, robbers and wild beasts couldn't get at them as easily. After the Passover, Mary and Joseph joined their friends and neighbors and headed back toward Nazareth. They thought Jesus was with some other people in the group. But He wasn't. Jesus had stayed behind in Jerusalem.

After a day on the road, Mary and Joseph searched the whole company. When they couldn't find Jesus, they hurried back to Jerusalem. For three days they looked and looked. No Jesus.

Finally they went to the temple, and there He was, sitting with the teachers, listening to them, and asking them questions. The

teachers were all very impressed with how intelligent this 12-year-old boy was.

But Jesus' parents were full of other kinds of feelings.

"My child!" cried Mary when she saw Him. "Why have You done this? See how worried Your father and I are? We've been looking everywhere for You!"

"Why were you looking for Me?" asked Jesus. "Didn't you know that I had to be busy with My Father's work?"

Mary and Joseph didn't understand what He meant at all.

Then Jesus got up and went back to Nazareth with them. The Bible doesn't tell us any more about His growing-up years, except to say that He obeyed His mother and father and grew wise and well-liked by everybody. ■

Luke 2:41-52

A Place to Be

Most kids I know
don't spend much time at church
talking with the teachers.
I wonder why Jesus did it.
Maybe He knew something we don't know.
Maybe He knew that the church
is a good place to grow,
to figure out who—or whose—you are,
to think about what you will do with your life.
Maybe I should try it, Father.
I can think of a couple of people
who would probably be glad
to talk with me.
Maybe I *will* try it!
What do You think, Father?

Jesus Is Baptized

Finally the time came for John to begin his work. He stayed in the wilderness and preached to anyone who would listen.

"Repent!" he said. "Turn around! God's kingdom is close at hand!"

Now John was a rough sort of man. He wore a robe made of camel's hair, with a leather belt around the middle; he ate nothing but locusts and wild honey. But word of his preaching spread, and people from all over came to hear him. They confessed their sins and John baptized them in the Jordan River.

One time John saw some church leaders coming to be baptized.

"You nest of snakes!" he cried. "Who told you to come here? If you are sorry for your sins, show it. But don't try to get by with pretending you're better than everyone else. You're not! Besides, I can just baptize you with water; but someone is coming after me, and He is more powerful than I am. I'm not fit even to take off His sandal. He will baptize you with the Holy Spirit and with fire."

Then Jesus came, all the way from Galilee, to be baptized by John.

"Oh, no!" said John. "I can't do that. I'm the one who needs to be baptized by You. And here You've come to me!"

"Let it be this way," said Jesus. "It is right that you baptize Me."

So John gave in and baptized Jesus. And as soon as Jesus came out of the water, heaven opened and God's Spirit came down in the form of a dove.

Then a voice spoke from heaven and said, "This is My beloved Son. My blessing is on Him." ◼

Matthew 3

The Same Thing

Jesus was baptized, Father,
by an ordinary human being.
I don't know why He had to do that.
But it's wonderful to know
that He was baptized just as I was.
And when I was, Father,
You "announced" in front of everybody,
just as You did for Jesus:
"You are My child.
My blessing is on you."

Jesus in the Wilderness

After Jesus was baptized, God's Spirit led Him out into the wilderness. For 40 days and 40 nights He went without food. Then, when He was very hungry, the devil came to Him.

"Listen," said the devil, "if You are really God's Son, tell these stones here to turn into bread."

But Jesus couldn't be fooled that easily.

"Scripture says that we do not live by bread alone," He said. "We live by every word that comes from God's mouth."

So the devil tried his second plan. He took Jesus to Jerusalem and had Him stand on the highest part of the temple.

"If You are really God's Son," he said, "jump. After all, Scripture says that God will have His angels take care of You. They will hold You with their hands; so You won't even hurt Your foot on a stone."

"That's right," said Jesus. "But Scripture also says that you should not test God."

Still the devil wasn't ready to give up. He took Jesus to a high mountain and showed Him all the kingdoms of the world.

"I'll give You all of these," he said, "if You'll just fall down at my feet and worship me."

Then Jesus said, "Get out of here, Satan! Scripture says, 'You must worship the Lord your God and Him only must you serve.'"

Well, the devil was defeated, so he left Jesus. And at once God sent angels to care for His Son. ■

Matthew 4:1-11

Prayer

I wish I could see the devil, Father.
I'd sure tell him what I think of him!
He's been causing trouble for thousands
of years!
The only problem is
he probably wouldn't look like the devil
if I did see him.
He wouldn't have horns and a tail
or carry a pitchfork.
He'd be too sneaky.
He'd look like another kid.
Or maybe he wouldn't look like anything.
Maybe he'd just be a little voice in my mind.
He's sneaky like that, isn't he, Father?
Why, before I figured out who he was,
I might end up doing what he suggested.
Maybe I even have.
There's only one way I can get that devil,
Father,
and that's with the strength I get from You.

Amen.

Jesus Calls Some Disciples

After Jesus came back from the wilderness, He returned to the area where John was teaching and baptizing. When John saw Jesus, he said to two of his disciples, "There is the Lamb of God."

When the two disciples, Andrew and John, heard this, they left John and followed Jesus. Later Andrew found his brother Simon and brought him to Jesus, saying, "We have found the Christ." When Jesus met Simon He changed his name to Peter, which means "rock." That is the name we know him by in most Bible stories.

Two other disciples, Philip and Nathanael also joined Jesus at this time.

This was the beginning of Jesus' ministry. He began traveling around and teaching people about God's love for them. Part of the time Jesus' new disciples were with Him and part of the time they spent at their regular jobs. Apparently Jesus did not ask His disciples to become His steady companions right away.

One day, about a year or so later, Jesus was standing beside the Sea of Galilee. A huge crowd had gathered to hear Him and kept pressing Him closer and closer to the edge of the water.

Jesus turned around and saw two boats not very far from shore. The fishermen weren't in them anymore. They were busy washing their nets. So Jesus got into one of the boats and began to teach the crowd from there.

Now the boat Jesus was in belonged to Peter, and when Jesus had finished teaching, He turned to Him.

"Take your boat out into the deep water," He said, "and let down your nets for a catch."

"Master," said Peter, "we've worked hard all night and didn't catch a thing. But if You say so, I'll take the boat out and let down the nets."

Night really was the best time for fishing, and if Peter hadn't caught anything then, the chances were good that he wouldn't catch anything during the day. But somehow he couldn't help trusting Jesus. So he and Andrew took their boat out into the deep water and lowered their nets.

At once they caught so many fish that their nets began to tear. They had to call to their partners, John and his brother James, to bring out their boat and help them. By the time the fish were all loaded, the two boats were so full that they almost sank.

Then Peter fell down in front of Jesus.

"Leave me, Lord!" he said. "I am a sinful man."

"Don't be afraid," said Jesus. "From now on you will be catching people."

And just like that Peter and Andrew and James and John left everything they owned, and followed Jesus. ∎

John 1:35-51
Luke 5:1-11

Traveling Light

Just like that
those guys dropped whatever they were doing
and followed Jesus.
They didn't worry about their jobs
or insurance policies or bank accounts
or what people would think
or any of that stuff.
They just followed
and traveled light.
Boy, I sure would like to get rid of
some of the stuff that's weighing me down.
Fears weigh a lot, Father,
and so do worries.
I'd like to drop them
and just follow Him.
I'd like to travel light.

Jesus' First Miracle

Soon after the disciples met Jesus for the first time, there was a wedding in the town of Cana in Galilee. Mary, Jesus' mother, was there, and Jesus and His disciples had been invited too.

Now back then a steward, who was sort of a head servant, often ran things for a family. That's the way it was at this wedding too, only a terrible thing happened. They ran out of wine. This would make everyone think the bridegroom hadn't bought enough to begin with, and he'd be horribly embarrassed.

When Mary found out what had happened, she went to Jesus and said, "They have no wine."

"Why do you turn to Me?" asked Jesus. "My hour has not come yet."

Then Mary said to the servants, "Do whatever He tells you to."

There were six stone jugs for water standing there, and each one could hold 20 or 30 gallons of water.

"Fill the jars with water," Jesus said to the servants, and they filled them—all the way up to the top.

"Now take some out," said Jesus, "and let the steward taste it."

The steward didn't know anything about what Jesus had done. He just tasted what the servants brought him and his mouth fell open with surprise.

"Come here!" he said to the bridegroom. "I don't understand this. Most people serve the best wine first and save the cheap kind till later. But you've kept the best till last!"

Jesus had changed the water into wine. His disciples knew it too, and from then on they believed more firmly in Him. ■

John 2:1-11

A Little Thing

I'm not sure I understand that story, Father,
not completely.
I'm not sure what Jesus meant
when He said that to His mother
and then changed the water into wine anyway.
But I think I understand one thing.
Jesus really cared about people.

He didn't want that bridegroom
to be embarrassed.
He didn't want the party to be a flop.
That might seem like a little thing
when we stop to think about the
important work
You sent Jesus to do.
But He knew it wasn't little
—not to those people.
So He worked His first miracle
and made the people happy.
He made His disciples happy too,
because they got something more than wine.
They got a little peek at who He really was.
And that was a big thing for them
—just as it is for me!

The Woman at the Well

One day Jesus made a trip from Judea to Galilee. To do that, He had to cross through the land of Samaria. Jesus was feeling pretty tired when He got to the Samaritan town of Sychar. So while His disciples went on into the town to buy food, He stopped by a well to rest.

While He was there, a Samaritan woman came out of the town to get some water from the well.

"Give Me a drink," Jesus said to her.

"What?" said the woman. "You, a Jew, are asking a Samaritan woman for a drink?" In those days the Jewish people didn't think much of the Samaritan people and wouldn't have anything to do with them.

"If you only knew what God is offering you," said Jesus. "If you only knew who is asking you for a drink. Then you would have been the one to do the asking, and I would have given you living water."

"Sir, You don't have a bucket," said the woman, "and the well is deep. How would You get this living water?"

"Whoever drinks *this* water will just get thirsty again," said Jesus. "But whoever drinks the water I shall give will never be thirsty again. My water will give you eternal life."

"Sir, I would like to have some of that water," said the woman.

"Go and call your husband," said Jesus. "Then come back here.

"I have no husband," said the woman.

"You're right," said Jesus. "Although you've had five husbands, the man you're living with now is not your husband."

"I can tell You are a prophet, Sir," said the woman. "Our ancestors used to worship in this place, even though you Jews say people ought to worship in Jerusalem."

"Someday you will worship the Father neither here nor in Jerusalem," said Jesus. "God is a spirit and you must worship Him in spirit and in truth."

The woman wasn't quite sure what Jesus was talking about. But she didn't give up.

"I know that one day God will send a Savior," she said. "He will explain everything to us."

"I am He," said Jesus.

Just then His disciples came back. They were surprised to find Him talking to this Samaritan woman, but they didn't say anything.

The woman put down her water jar and ran back to town. "Come!" she said to everyone she met. "Come and see a man who has told me everything I've ever done. I wonder if He really is the Savior."

Many people left the town and followed the woman back to the well.

Meanwhile, Jesus' disciples were trying to get Him to eat something.

"I have food that you don't know anything about," Jesus told them.

"What is He talking about?" the disciples asked one another. "Has someone else been bringing Him food?"

"No," said Jesus. "My food is to do God's work. Look around. The fields are ready to be harvested. The reaper is already bringing in the grain for eternal life. I have sent you to reap the crops that others have planted."

By then the townspeople had reached Jesus.

"Please, come into our town and stay for a while," they begged Him.

So Jesus stayed with them for two days and taught them about God's kingdom. Many began to believe in Him. "We know now that He really is the Savior," they said. ∎

John 4:1-42

Prayer

"The fields are ready to be harvested."
It was people Jesus was talking about,
wasn't it, Father?
People were ready to learn about Him,
to learn who He was
and what He could do for them.
They still are,
aren't they, Father?
There are people all around us
who are ready for Jesus
—a whole big crop of them.
Help me tell them.
Help me show them.
I don't want to turn them off
and that's easy to do these days.
So You help me, Father.
Make me Your reaper.

Amen.

The Nobleman's Son

After Jesus left the Samaritan town, He went back to Cana, where He had changed the water into wine. Now there was a man there, a court official, whose son was sick in Capernaum. When he heard that Jesus was in town, he rushed to see Him.

"Sir, please come and cure my son," he begged. "He is about to die."

"Won't you believe without signs?" asked Jesus. But the man was too worried about his son to understand what Jesus meant.

"Please, Sir, come before my child dies!" he pleaded.

"Go home," said Jesus. "Your son will live."

The man believed Jesus and started for home. While he was still on the way, he met some of his servants. They had come to find him.

"Master, your son is alive!" they cried.

"When did he begin to get better?" asked the man.

"Yesterday, at the seventh hour," they said.

"That is exactly the time Jesus said he would live!" exclaimed the man.

And from then on he and everyone in his house believed in Jesus. ■

John 4:46-53

Prayer

That man did need a sign.
He needed to hear Jesus say,
"Your son will live."
But then he believed
and so did everyone in his house.

It would be better,
wouldn't it, Father,
if we could believe without signs?
But we're awfully weak that way.
Well, You sent us the best sign of all.
You let Your Son die for us
and You made Him alive again.
That's quite a sign.
Help us see it!

Amen.

Jesus Goes Home

After that, Jesus went back to His own hometown of Nazareth. On the Sabbath, He went to the synagog the way He usually did. He was asked to read the lesson.

Jesus stood up and someone brought Him the scroll that contained the writings of the prophet Isaiah. Jesus unrolled the scroll and found the part He wanted to read.

"God's Spirit is upon Me," He read, "because He has anointed Me. He has sent Me to bring good news to the poor, to announce freedom to the captives, to give sight to the blind, to set oppressed people free, and to proclaim the year of the Lord."

Jesus rolled up the scroll, handed it back to the attendant, and sat back down. Everyone was watching Him, and He began to talk to them.

"These words that Isaiah wrote are coming true right now while you are listening," He said.

Everyone was amazed.

"Isn't this Joseph's son?" they asked.

"You've probably heard about the things I did in Capernaum," Jesus continued. "And you might think that I should do the same

sorts of things here in My own territory. But prophets are never accepted in their own country.

"There were a lot of widows in Israel in the days when Elijah was alive. But God didn't send Elijah to any of them. He sent Elijah to a foreign widow. There were many lepers in Israel when Elisha was alive. But God didn't have Elisha cure any of them. He had him cure Naaman, a foreigner.

When the people heard Jesus saying these things, they were furious. They jumped to their feet, pushed Him out of town, took Him to the top of a hill, and tried to throw Him off. But Jesus slipped out of their hands and walked away. ■

Luke 4:16-30

Prayer

That must have hurt Jesus
—to have the people in His own hometown
turn against Him and even try to kill Him.
He was only telling them the truth,
but I guess they didn't want to hear that.
People don't sometimes.
The truth makes them mad.
I hope nothing like that ever happens to me,
Father.
I know it would hurt me a lot.
But You'll let Your Spirit be with me too,
won't You, Father?
Just as He was with Jesus?
I'll be okay then.
And, Father,
help me listen to the truth
better than those people did.

Amen.

Jesus Heals a Paralyzed Man

Jesus performed many miracles. Most often He made sick people well. After a while, people began coming to Him wherever He was and asking Him to heal them.

One day Jesus was in a house in Capernaum, teaching God's Word. The house was so full of people listening to Him that there was no room left at all, not even in front of the door.

Along came four men, carrying a paralyzed man on a stretcher. He was their friend, and they wanted Jesus to heal him. But the crowd was so huge that they couldn't get the paralyzed man anywhere near Jesus.

So they climbed onto the roof of the house, made a hole right above where Jesus was standing, and lowered their friend down through the hole on his stretcher.

When Jesus saw how strong their faith in Him was, He said to the paralyzed man, "My child, your sins are forgiven."

Now there were some church leaders in the house, and they didn't like what Jesus said. "How can He say something like that?" they thought. "Only God can forgive sins."

Jesus knew what they were thinking. "Why are you thinking these things?" He asked them. "Is it easier to say, 'Your sins are forgiven' or 'Pick up your stretcher and walk'? But if I have to prove to you that I have the power to forgive sins, I will."

He turned to the paralyzed man. "Get up," He said. "Pick up your stretcher and go home."

At once the man did it. Everyone was so amazed that all they could do was praise God and say, "We've never seen anything like this before!" ■

Mark 2:1-12

Prayer

Why did they doubt Him, Father?
Couldn't those leaders *tell* that Jesus was special?
He *did* work all those miracles right in front of them.
Those guys must have been stupid
—just as I am sometimes.
After all, I *know* who Jesus is.
I know a lot more about Him than those guys did.
And I still doubt Him sometimes.
I let myself get all messed up
with worries and fears and guilts

and I don't even bother to ask Him for help.
That's stupid!
Help me get smart, Father.
Help me remember what I already know.
Help me turn to Jesus
again and again.
He'll be there!

Amen.

Matthew

One day Jesus was walking along with a bunch of people who were listening to Him talk about God. As He walked, He saw a man called Matthew, sitting by the customs house. Now Matthew was a tax collector and tax collectors weren't very popular back then. A lot of them cheated and took more money than they were supposed to from the people.

Jesus didn't pay any attention to any of that, though. He looked right at Matthew and said, "Follow Me."

At once Matthew got up and followed Him.

Later Jesus and His disciples went to dinner at Matthew's house. A bunch of other tax collectors were there too and so were some other people whom everyone knew had done bad things.

Some of the church leaders found out about the dinner and decided to have a talk with Jesus' disciples.

"Why does Jesus eat with tax collectors and sinners?" they asked.

Jesus heard them. "It isn't healthy people who need a doctor," He said. "It's sick people. I did not come to call people who do everything right. I came to call sinners."

That wasn't the only time the church leaders scolded Jesus for the way He behaved. Back then good church people would go without food for long periods of time. This was called fasting.

"Why don't Your disciples fast too?" the church leaders asked Jesus.

"Nobody fasts when the bridegroom is with them," said Jesus. "They wait until after He's gone. They're too happy to fast while He is with them."

Another time Jesus and His disciples were walking through some cornfields on the

Sabbath. The Sabbath was every Saturday and on that day people weren't supposed to do any work.

But the disciples picked some ears of corn as they were walking, and the church leaders thought this counted as work.

"Why are Your disciples doing that?" they asked Jesus.

"The Sabbath was made for people," said Jesus. "People weren't made for the Sabbath. And the Son of Man is Master even over the Sabbath." The Son of Man was a special name for the Savior God promised to send.

But the church leaders still didn't understand. Jesus went into a synagog and saw a man whose hand was crippled.

"Now what is He going to do?" said the church leaders to themselves. "If He heals that man, He'll be working on the Sabbath."

"Is it wrong to do something good on the Sabbath?" Jesus asked them. "Or is it wrong to do something evil? Is it wrong to save a life? Or is it wrong to kill?"

The church leaders wouldn't even speak to Him, and this made Jesus sad and angry all at once.

"Stretch out your hand," He said to the man.

The man did, and at once his hand was better.

Out marched the church leaders, muttering and sputtering. "We have to get rid of this Jesus," they said. ■

Mark 2:13—3:6

Rules

Rules!
People think there have to be rules
for everything, Father.
They don't know what to do without them.
If you follow all the rules,
you're okay.
If you break one,
too bad for you!
I guess rules are okay sometimes.
They make things work better sometimes.
But some things are just too big for rules
—like Your love
and Your Son.

Jesus' Mountaintop Sermon

One day Jesus sat on a hill and preached a powerful sermon. We call it the Sermon on the Mount. In this sermon Jesus said some things that must have sounded strange to the people who heard them. He was talking about the way life is in God's kingdom, and people weren't used to hearing about that.

"Happy are the poor in spirit," He said. "God's kingdom belongs to them. Happy are the gentle. The earth will belong to them. Happy are those who cry. They will be comforted. Happy are those who want what is right more than anything else. They will get what they want. Happy are those who are kind and forgiving toward others. They will get kindness and forgiveness in return. Happy are those whose hearts are pure. They will see God. Happy are those who work for peace. They will be called God's children. Happy are those who get in trouble for trying to do what is right. God's kingdom belongs to them.

"You are the salt of the earth. But if salt loses its taste, it is useless. Nothing can make it salty again.

"You are the light of the world. Nobody buys a lamp and then puts it under a basket. They put it on a table so it will give light for everyone in the house. You must let your light shine that way. When people see the good things you do, they will praise God, your Father.

"There is a saying that goes, 'Love your neighbor and hate your enemy.' Well, I say you should love your enemies and pray for those who do evil things to you. When you do this, you will be acting like God's children.

"And don't be a showoff about the good things you do. Don't tell everyone how much money you give to the poor. Don't even let your left hand know how much money your right hand gives. God will reward you.

"And don't be a showoff when you pray either. Don't stand up and shout your prayers in front of everyone, so they'll think you're religious. Pray to God and He will reward you. And here is a prayer you can say:

"Our Father, who art in heaven,
hallowed be Thy name.
Thy kingdom come,
Thy will be done
on earth as it is in heaven.
Give us this day our daily bread

and forgive us our trespasses
as we forgive those who trespass
against us.
Lead us not into temptation,
but deliver us from evil.

"Don't worry about your life or what you're going to eat or what you're going to wear. Look at the birds! They don't plant seeds or harvest crops, but God takes care of them. Aren't you worth more than they are? And look at the flowers. They don't make clothes for themselves, but even Solomon didn't have such beautiful things to wear as they do. Aren't you worth more than flowers. God knows what you need. Make His kingdom the most important thing in your lives and He'll take care of all the rest." ■

Matthew 5:1—6:34

Prayer

"Happy are the poor in spirit."
"Happy are those who cry."
It's all turned around, Father,
that world Your Son describes.
Everything's backward and upside-down.
Nothing makes sense at all,
except . . .
except when I remember
that Jesus is talking about Your kingdom.
And Your kingdom isn't like the world,
is it, Father?
Even though it's right here *in* the world,
it's different.
It's so different that miracles happen
and shepherds become kings
and Your Son is born in a stable
and death is killed forever.
Your kingdom is different all right, Father,
and how happy I am that I live there!

Amen.

The Centurion's Servant

After Jesus' great sermon, He went to Capernaum and a centurion came to him. A centurion was a Roman officer who was in charge of 100 soldiers.

"Sir," said the centurion to Jesus, "my servant at home is very ill. He can't move, and he is in terrible pain."

"I will come and make him well," said Jesus.

"Sir," said the centurion, "I am not good enough to have You in my house. Just say the word and my servant will be well. I know what it means to be in charge of things. I have a lot of soldiers under me, and if I tell one of them to go someplace, he does it. If I tell another one to come to me, he does it. You have even more power than that."

Jesus was astonished by what the man said and turned to His disciples.

"I have never seen anyone with faith like this," He said, "not even in Israel. Many other people will come from far places too and be part of God's kingdom."

Then Jesus turned back to the centurion.

"Go home then," He said. "You have believed, and I will do this thing for you."

The centurion went home and found out that his servant got well the very minute Jesus said those words. ■

Matthew 8:5-13

Faith

That officer *believed*, Father.
He didn't even have to see
Jesus work a miracle.
He *knew* Jesus could do it.
And of course Jesus did.
Maybe that's what faith is
—knowing something without seeing it.
I wish I had faith like that.
There is so much, though,
I can't see or don't understand.
I *want* to believe, Father,
but sometimes I have trouble.
Faith is one of those gifts
that comes from You, isn't it, Father?

A Widow's Son

Not long after Jesus made the centurion's servant well, He went to a town called Nain. His disciples and a lot of other people who loved to be with Him went with Him.

When they were almost to the gate of the town, they saw a funeral procession. A dead man was being carried out to be buried. His mother was walking along beside the body, and so were many of the townspeople. The mother's husband was already dead, and now that her son had died too, she had no one left. Jesus felt sorry for her.

"Don't cry," He said to her.

Then He went up to the stretcher that the body lay on and touched it. At once the people carrying it stopped.

"Young man," said Jesus, "I tell you to get up."

Just like that the dead man sat up and began to talk.

"Here is your son," said Jesus to the woman.

Of course everyone was amazed. They began to praise God.

"This is a great prophet!" they said. "God has visited His people!"

News of this miracle got around fast, and many people began to talk about what a great prophet Jesus was. ■

Luke 7:11-17

Prayer

I guess it's hard to die, Father.
But it's hard to be left behind too.
You take care of those who have died
and they're all right.
But we miss them so much.
I think Jesus knew that, Father.
The story doesn't say He made
the young man alive
because *he* wanted to be alive.
It says Jesus felt sorry for the mother,
and He gave her son back to her.
That makes me feel good.
It helps me know that You care
about the people who are left behind too,
the people who hurt so much
from missing someone.

Be with them now too, Father.
Comfort them and let Your love
make them strong.

Amen.

The Woman and the Oil

One day one of the church leaders invited Jesus to his house for a meal. While Jesus was sitting at the table, a woman came in. Everyone in town knew that she was a bad person. But she had heard that Jesus was going to be at this man's house, and so she came to see Him. With her she brought an alabaster jar of precious ointment.

Before anyone could stop her, she fell at Jesus' feet, weeping. Her tears fell on His feet and she wiped them away with her hair. Then she kissed His feet and rubbed the precious ointment on them.

When the church leader saw what was going on, he thought to himself, "If this Jesus really were a prophet, He'd know what kind of woman she is!"

"I have something to say to you, Simon," said Jesus.

"Speak, Master," said Simon.

"Once there was a man to whom two other men owed some money. One of them owed him 500 denarii and the other owed him 50 denarii. Neither one of them was able to pay him back, so the man told them both to forget it. Which one do you think loved him more?"

"The one who owed him more, I suppose," said Simon.

"Right," said Jesus. Then He turned to the woman, "Simon, do you see this woman?" He asked. I came into your house, and you didn't pour any water over My feet, even though that is the custom. But she poured her own tears over My feet and wiped them with her hair. You didn't anoint My head with oil, even though that is the custom. But she anointed My feet with precious ointment. She must know that all of her sins have been forgiven or she wouldn't show such great love for Me. It's the people who haven't had much forgiven who show little love.

"Woman," He continued, "your sins *are* forgiven."

This really confused the other people at the table.

"Who is He that He can forgive sins?" they wondered.

But Jesus didn't pay any attention to them.

"Go in peace," He said to the woman. "Your faith has saved you." ■

Luke 7:36-50

Prayer

Why do people always have to be
putting other people down?
Why do they always have to feel
superior to other people?
Is it because inside
they really feel like nobodies themselves?
Do they hurt others
just to make themselves feel better?
I hate that, Father,
and I hope I never do it.
Jesus made it pretty clear
who He came to help
—the people who are put down,
the people who know they're nobodies.
I don't mind admitting
that I'm one of those people, Father.
There are a lot of things wrong with me.
But Jesus came to make me brand new,
so I'm all right!

Amen.

The Story of the Seeds

One day Jesus was teaching beside a big lake. After a while, the crowd listening to Him got so big that He had to get into a boat and teach from there.

One of the ways Jesus taught was by telling the people stories called parables. These parables described what life was like in God's kingdom. Sitting in the boat, Jesus told the people a parable:

"Picture a man going out to plant some seeds," He said. In those days people planted seeds by scattering handfuls of them across a field.

"As this man planted his seeds, some of them fell on the edge of the path. Along came the birds and ate them up. Some other seeds fell on rocky ground. They grew, but there wasn't much dirt for them, so they couldn't put down long roots. When the sun came out, the little plants burned up. Their tiny roots couldn't get enough water for them.

"Other seeds fell into a thorny place. They tried to grow, but the thorns choked them and they died. And some seeds fell into good rich soil. They grew into tall strong plants and produced much grain. Listen, everyone who has ears to hear!"

Later, Jesus' disciples asked Him what this parable meant.

"Don't you understand?" He asked. "The man is planting God's word. The seeds that fall on the edge of the path are like people

who hear God's word but let the devil make them forget it right away. The seeds that fall on rocky ground are like people who are very happy when they first hear God's word. But as soon as the going gets rough, they forget about it.

"The seeds that fall among thorns are like people who hear God's word, but let all the things of this world—worries and riches and things like that—choke it. And the seeds that fall into good rich soil are like people who hear God's word and accept it. They grow tall and strong and produce a good crop of God's love." ∎

Mark 4:1-20

Prayer

What a neat way to teach about Your kingdom, Father!
Jesus painted word-pictures of what it was like,
so the people could hear and understand.
I like that picture of the man planting seeds,
and I hope I'm like one of the seeds that fell into good rich soil.
But if I'm not, Father,
if I get a little too close
to the edge of the path
or the rocks or the thorns,
help me scoot over
to where I ought to be
I want to produce a good crop of Your love.

Amen.

More Stories

Jesus told other stories about God's kingdom too.

"God's kingdom," He said, "is like yeast. A woman takes just a little bit of it and mixes it with lots and lots of flour. And just that little bit of yeast is enough to make all the flour rise.

"The kingdom of God is like a treasure hidden in a field. Someone finds it and then hides it again right away. Then he rushes off, sells everything he owns, and buys the field so the treasure is his forever.

"The kingdom of God is like a businessman looking for fine pearls. When he finds an especially valuable one, he sells everything else he owns so he can buy it.

"The kingdom of God is like a mustard seed. When you plant it, it is the smallest seed of all. But after it is planted, it grows and grows until it is a huge shrub. Big branches grow from its trunk and the birds settle on them and rest in the shade." ■

Matthew 13:33, 44-46;
Mark 4:30-32

Prayer

Jesus said Your kingdom
is like a mustard seed, Father.
It's very tiny to start
but it grows and it grows till it's huge.
Well, Jesus started with just 12 disciples
and look at His church now!
Is that what He meant?
Maybe that's part of it.
But I think He meant something else too.
I think He meant what happens to people
once they start living in Your kingdom.
At first their lives change just a tiny bit.
But You keep working on them, Father,
until by the time You're finished,
they're whole new people.
I think that's neat!

Amen.

54

Jesus and the Storm

When evening came, Jesus said to His disciples, "Let's cross over to the other side of the lake."

So some of them got into the boat with Him, others got into other boats, and they all set out across the lake.

Jesus was exhausted from all the teaching He'd done, so He curled up in the back of the boat, put His head on a cushion, and fell asleep.

And then a storm came up. A fierce wind blew, and huge waves began to slap against the side of the boat. After a while the waves even splashed into the boat until it seemed ready to sink.

"Master, wake up!" cried His disciples. "Don't You even care what's going on? Our boat is sinking!"

Jesus woke up and scolded the wind. Then He said to the sea, "Calm down! Be quiet now!"

At once the wind dropped and the sea grew calm.

Then Jesus turned to His disciples. "Why are you so scared?" He asked. "Why don't you have any faith?"

Their mouths dropped open and they turned to one another.

"Who is He?" they asked. "Even the wind and the sea do what He says!" ■

Mark 4:35-41

Prayer

I wouldn't have been scared, Father.
No matter how high the waves got,
if Jesus was in my boat
I'd be brave as anything
—I think.
Of course I *say* I believe
that Jesus is with me now.
And that doesn't always stop me
from getting scared.
Is it another one of those faith things, Father?
Am I sometimes as scared as the
disciples were?
We both know the answer to that, Father.
Help me trust in You.

Amen.

The Man at the Burial Caves

Jesus and His disciples reached the other side of the lake and left their boats. They'd no sooner stepped onto the shore, though, when a man came toward them from the burial caves.

This man was possessed by an evil spirit. He lived in the caves and no one could do a thing with him. People had tried to hold him down with chains, but he was so strong that he broke them and ran away again.

All day and all night he wandered around the caves and in the mountains, howling and cutting himself with stones.

When he saw Jesus, he came running up to Him and fell at His feet.

"What do You want with me, Jesus?" he shouted. "You are the Son of the Most High God. Swear by Him that You will not torture me!"

Jesus did not talk to the man. Instead He talked to the evil spirit within him.

"Come out of that man," He said. "What is your name?"

"My name is Legion," said the spirit. "There are many of us. Please, don't send us away from here."

Nearby was a great herd of 2,000 pigs, feeding on the side of the mountain.

"Send us to the pigs!" begged the spirits. "Let us go into them."

"All right," said Jesus.

At once the spirits came out of the man and went into the pigs. All 2,000 pigs charged off a cliff into the lake, and there they were drowned.

The men who had been taking care of the pigs couldn't believe it. They ran to town and told their story to everyone. Soon many people came out to the lake to see what had really happened. When they got there, they saw the man from the tombs sitting quietly, perfectly well. And they were afraid.

"Go away from here, please," they said to Jesus.

So He started to get into His boat.

"Wait!" cried the man from the caves. "I want to go with You. Please let me!"

"No," said Jesus. "You must go home to your own people. Tell them all that the Lord has done for you."

So the man went off and began to tell people what Jesus had done for him. And everyone who heard was amazed. ■

Mark 5:1-20

Safe

What are the evil spirits, Father?
Are they like devils
who go around getting into people?
Can that really happen?
It sure is scary to think about.
I guess what I've got to remember is that
Jesus was stronger than those evil spirits.
He threw them out
and the man was well again.
Jesus is stronger than *anything*,

isn't He, Father?
So I don't have to worry about evil spirits
or any of that other scary stuff.
As long as Jesus is with me,
I'm safe.

Two More Miracles

When Jesus got back to the other side of the lake again, another crowd of people met Him and gathered around Him. So He stayed there for a while to teach them.

Then a church leader, a man called Jairus, came up to Him and fell at His feet.

"Jesus," he said, "my little girl is terribly sick. Please come, lay Your hands on her, and make her better. It will save her life!"

So Jesus went with him and the crowd went too, pressing all around Jesus.

Now in the crowd was a woman who had been ill for many years. She had paid a lot of money to many doctors and suffered all sorts of painful treatments. But she still wasn't any better. In fact, she was getting worse. She had heard about Jesus, though, and so she came up behind Him and touched His cloak.

"If I can just touch His clothes," she said to herself, "I will be well again." And she was.

At once Jesus turned around. "Who touched my clothes?" He asked.

"Jesus, there are many people around You," said His disciples. "How can You ask who touched Your clothes?"

But Jesus kept looking around and at last the woman came forward, shaking and scared. She fell at Jesus' feet and told Him the whole story.

"My daughter," He said, "your faith has made you well. Go in peace now."

While He was still talking, some people arrived from Jairus' house.

"Don't bother Jesus anymore," they said to Jairus. "Your daughter is dead."

"Don't be afraid, Jairus," said Jesus. "Just have faith."

He went on to Jairus' house, but the only people He let go with Him were Peter, James, John, and Jairus.

When they got to the house, they found the people there sobbing and wailing. Jesus went in and said to them, "Why are you making all this noise? The little girl isn't dead. She's asleep."

But they laughed at Him. *They* knew the girl was dead.

So Jesus told them all to leave. Then He took His own three disciples and the girl's mother and father and went into the place where she was lying. He took her by the hand and said, *"Talitha, kumi!"* That means, "Little girl, get up!" in Aramean.

At once the little girl got up and began to walk around. Her parents just stood there, astonished.

"I think you'd better give her something to eat," said Jesus. ■

Mark 5:21-43

Prayer

It's another story of faith, Father.
That woman who touched Jesus' clothes believed that He could heal her without words.
I'll bet she wasn't even surprised when He did
—just glad.
I don't know if I can *ever* have faith like that, Father.
But I like to read about people who did.
It's sort of like taking lessons in faith.
Thank You for those people.

Amen.

The Death of John

King Herod—a different Herod from the one who ordered the babies killed when Jesus was born—had married his brother Philip's wife, Herodias. Now this was against the law, and John told Herod so. Herodias was furious about this and wanted to have John killed. But Herod was too frightened of John to kill him. He knew John was a good and holy man, so he had John shut up in prison instead, where he would be safe. Sometimes Herod even listened to John speak, but he could not decide what to do with him.

While John was in prison, he heard about the things that Jesus was doing and sent some of his own disciples to see Jesus.

"John wants to know if you are the Savior God promised," they said. "Or do we have to wait for someone else?"

"Tell John what you have seen," said Jesus. "Tell him that the blind can see and the lame can walk. Tell him that lepers are made well, the deaf can hear, the dead are raised to life, and the poor are told Good News. Happy are those who do not lose faith in Me."

After John's disciples left, Jesus turned to the crowd. "Who did you go out in the wilderness to see?" He asked them. "A man wearing fine clothes? No, you went to hear a prophet. And John is far more than a prophet. He is the one God sent to prepare the way for the Lord."

Meanwhile, King Herod's birthday rolled around, and he gave a big party for all the important people in town. As part of the entertainment, Herodias' daughter, a young woman called Salome, came in and danced.

Herod and his guests thought she did a great job, and Herod told her she could have anything she wanted—even half his kingdom—for her reward.

Salome ran right out to her mother. "What shall I ask for?" she said.

"Ask for John's head," said Herodias.

Salome went straight back to the king. "I want John's head," she said. "I want it right now and I want it on a dish."

Herod was horrified. But he thought about the promise he'd made and all the guests who'd heard him make it, and he couldn't figure out any way to get out of keeping it. So he sent one of his bodyguards off to the prison.

Soon the man came back with John's head. Herod gave it to Salome and she gave it to her mother.

When John's disciples found out what had happened, they got John's body and buried it in a tomb. ■

Matthew 11:2-10;
Mark 6:17-29

Prayer

That's a horrible story, Father.
Why would You let something like that
happen to one of Your people,
a man who spent His whole life serving You?
I don't understand.
It scares me and it makes me mad.
But I don't know what to do about it.
You are God, Father,
and You can do whatever You want.
All I can do is trust
that You are doing the best thing,
even when it doesn't look that way to me.
Maybe . . .
maybe it was easier for John to die
than to live much longer and see
what people would do to Jesus.
Oh, I don't know!
But maybe knowing isn't the
important thing.
Maybe trusting is.
I think I need some help from You.

Amen.

Jesus Feeds Some People

One day Jesus was sitting on a hillside, teaching His disciples. As usual, many people found Him and began coming closer to hear what He was saying.

"Where are we going to buy some bread for these people to eat?" Jesus asked His disciple Philip. He said this to test Philip. He knew exactly what He was going to do.

"We have 200 denarii," said Philip, "but that would not give them each a tiny piece of bread."

"There's a little boy here," said Andrew, Peter's brother. "He has five loaves of barley bread and two fish. But how much good will that do with so many people?"

"Make the people sit down," Jesus told His disciples.

There was plenty of grass on the hillside, and about 5,000 people sat down.

Then Jesus took the loaves of bread, thanked God for them, and gave them out to the people. He did the same thing with the fish. Everyone had plenty to eat.

After they were finished, Jesus told His disciples to pick up the leftovers, so nothing

would get wasted. They did, and they filled 12 baskets.

When the people saw all this, they said, "This really is the prophet God promised to send."

Jesus knew that they were going to try to make Him king by force, so He hurried away and hid in the hills by Himself. ■

John 6:1-15

Something Else

All those people!
No wonder they wanted to make Jesus king after He fed them.
That must have been an incredible thing to see.
I wonder just why Jesus did it.
Was it to show His disciples once again who He really was?
Was it to show everyone there?
I guess that was part of it,
although the people didn't understand very well.
They thought Jesus should be an earthly king.
But I think He wanted to show something else too, Father.
I think Jesus wanted everyone to know that You really care about hungry people.
You really want them to have enough to eat.
Your prophets said that again and again, but Jesus *showed* it.
We need to pay attention to that today, Father.
There are a lot of hungry people left.

Jesus Walks on Water

Right after Jesus fed the 5,000, He made His disciples get into a boat and go on ahead of Him to Bethsaida. He sent the crowd away, and then He went into the hills by Himself to pray.

When evening came, the boat with the disciples was way out on the lake, and Jesus was alone on land. He could tell that His disciples were worn out. They had been rowing against the wind, and that was hard work.

So Jesus went out toward them, walking on the water.

They all saw Him and at once thought He was a ghost. They were terrified and cried out.

"Courage!" said Jesus. "Don't be afraid. It is I."

He got into the boat and the wind stopped blowing. Now it would be easier to row.

But the disciples were speechless. They had just seen Jesus perform the miracle with the loaves and fish, but they hadn't understood what it meant. Now they had seen two more miracles. Yet because their faith was often weak, their understanding of who Jesus was, was still mixed up. ■

Mark 6:45-52

Prayer

If Jesus could walk on water,
what other things could He do, Father?
Why, if He'd wanted to,
He could have taken over the whole world!
He could have made lots of money
and bossed everyone around
and lived here forever.
But that wasn't what Jesus wanted.
He wanted to save us,
to show us Your love,
and make us Yours forever.

He took over the world all right.
But He did it the hard way —on a cross.
Father, I'm so glad He did.

Amen.

Peter Speaks Up

One day Jesus and His disciples left for the villages around Caesarea Philippi. On the way, Jesus asked His disciples a question.

"Who do people say I am?" He asked.

"Oh, some people say you are John the Baptist," they answered. "And others say You are the prophet Elijah. Still others say You're another one of the prophets."

"And how about you?" asked Jesus. "Who do you say I am?"

Then Peter spoke up. "You are the Christ," he said, "the One God promised to send."

"I'm giving you strict orders not to tell anyone this," said Jesus. Then He began to teach them about what was going to happen. He told them that He would suffer greatly. The church leaders would all be against Him, and He would be put to death. After three days, though, He would be alive again.

This upset Peter terribly, and he tried to tell Jesus that it wouldn't happen that way at all.

"Get behind Me, Satan!" Jesus said to him. "You are thinking like people, not like God!"

Then Jesus explained that the people who followed Him would have to carry crosses too. "That's what it will be like to follow Me," He said. "But if you lose your life, you will also save it. And if you are not ashamed of Me, then I will not be ashamed of you." ■

Mark 8:27-38

Prayer

Poor old Peter!
He put his foot right in his mouth,
didn't he, Father?
And right after he'd said that
wonderful thing
about who Jesus really was.
I understand Peter,
because I'm a lot like him.
I'm always putting my foot in my mouth too.
But it didn't make Jesus stop loving him
or letting him be a disciple.
That's good news,
because I want to go on following too,
even if I do mess up sometimes.
If it means a cross, Father,
that's okay.
Just don't let me ever be ashamed of Jesus.

Amen.

Jesus Is Transfigured

Six days after Peter said who Jesus was, Jesus took him and James and John up a high mountain where they could be alone. And while they were there, Jesus' clothes became a dazzling white, whiter than any bleach could ever make them. Jesus looked different too. He was transfigured.

Then the prophet Elijah appeared and so did Moses. They began talking with Jesus. The disciples didn't know what to think or say, but Peter decided he'd better say something.

"Teacher," he said to Jesus, "it's such a wonderful thing for us all to be here. Why don't we make three tents—one for You, one for Moses, and one for Elijah?"

Actually Peter was feeling pretty scared and so were James and John. They'd never seen anything like this before.

Then a bright cloud came and covered them all with its shadow. Out of the cloud came a voice.

"This is My Son, the Beloved," it said. "Listen to Him."

And suddenly the cloud was gone and so were Moses and Elijah. Only Jesus was still with them, and He led His three disciples back down the mountain. On the way down He told them not to tell anyone what happened until He had risen from the dead. ■

Mark 9:2-9

On the Mountain

Boy, would I like to have been
on that mountain,
to see Elijah and Moses,
and to hear Your voice, Father.

Of course, I probably would have messed up.
I'd have wanted to build some tents,
like Peter did,
or maybe have a party
or take a picture.
We humans get pretty shook
at times like that, holy times.
But, boy, would I like to have been there!
Well, instead I guess I'll do what You
said, Father.
I'll listen to Him,
Your beloved Son.
I'll listen through Your Word and the church.
And I guess in a way that's as good as
being there.

A Sick Boy

When Jesus, Peter, James, and John got back to the rest of the disciples, they found a big crowd of people around them. Some church leaders were arguing with them too. The minute everyone saw Jesus, they all ran to say hello to Him.

"What are you arguing about?" Jesus asked.

"Master, I have brought my little boy to You," said one man. "He has an evil spirit in him. When it takes hold, it throws him down on the ground. He foams at the mouth and grinds his teeth and gets stiff all over. I asked Your disciples to get rid of that evil spirit, but they couldn't do it."

"You people with no faith!" said Jesus. "How long am I going to have to put up with you? Bring that boy to Me."

They brought the boy to Jesus, and as soon as the evil spirit saw Jesus, it threw the boy into one of his fits. He lay on the ground, twisting and turning and foaming at the mouth.

"How long has he had this trouble?" Jesus asked the boy's father.

"Ever since he was a little child," said the father. "Sometimes the spirit even throws him into fire or into water. Please, if You can do anything, have pity on us. Help us!

"If you can believe," said Jesus, "everything is possible."

"I *do* have faith!" cried the man. "Maybe it isn't much, but please help the little bit I have!"

Then Jesus spoke to the evil spirit. "I order you to come out of that boy!" He said. "And don't ever go back into him again!"

With that, the spirit came out and the boy lay on the ground, as still as if he were dead.

"He is dead," said the people. "Look, he's dead!"

But Jesus took the boy's hand and helped him up. He was able to stand. He was well!

Later the disciples had a private talk with Jesus.

"Why couldn't we get rid of that evil spirit?" they asked.

"It is the kind of evil spirit that only prayer can get rid of," said Jesus. ■

Mark 9:14-29

Prayer

One minute He was on the mountain, Father, being transfigured,
and the next minute He was down
with the people again,
making a sick boy well.
I guess that's the way
You want us to live too.
Sometimes we'll feel high and holy and clean all over.
Other times we'll feel scared and dirty and caught in the pain of earth.
And You want us in both places, Father, worshiping You
and showing Your love to others.
Okay!
But please be with us.

Amen.

Taxes and a Fish

Then Jesus and His disciples traveled to Capernaum. While they were there, some tax collectors came up to Peter.

"Does your Master pay the tax He owes us or doesn't He?" they asked. They were talking about the tax money that was used to help take care of the temple.

"Oh, yes," said Peter and he hurried into the house.

But before he could say a word, Jesus said, "What do you think, Peter? Where do the kings on this earth get their tax money? Do they collect it from their own children or from foreigners?"

"They collect it from foreigners," said Peter.

"Well, that means their own children don't have to pay," said Jesus. He meant that He was God's Son and shouldn't have to pay to take care of God's temple.

"But," Jesus went on, "we don't want to make these collectors angry. So here's what I want you to do. Go to the lake and throw out a fishing line. Pull out the first fish that bites and look in its mouth. There you will find enough money to pay the tax. Give it to the collectors for Me and for you."

And that's exactly what Peter did. ∎

Matthew 17:24-27

Another Sign

I'll bet my folks would like
a fish like that
to pay their taxes every year.
I wouldn't mind having one myself!

Every time I wanted some money,
I'd just open that fish's mouth
and PLUNK!
There it'd be.
But I don't suppose the story
is really about fish and taxes,
is it, Father?

I think it's a story to tell us again
who that Jesus really is
—Your Son.
The fish was just a sign,
a way of showing us the truth.
Well, I guess Peter got the point and so do I.
Jesus is Your Son all right and I won't forget it!

Jesus and the Children

While Jesus and His disciples were in their house in Capernaum, Jesus turned to them and asked, "What were you arguing about while we were traveling here?"

The disciples didn't say a word. They had been arguing about which one of them was the greatest, and they were embarrassed for Jesus to know it. But He knew.

"Listen," He said, "whoever wants to be the first must think of being last. You must be the last of all and the servant of all."

There was a little child in the house, and Jesus put His arms around him and showed him to the disciples.

"Anyone who welcomes one of these little children in My name, welcomes Me," He said. "But whoever tries to hurt the faith of one of these little children—well—it would be better for that person to be thrown into the sea with a huge rock tied to him."

After that Jesus and His disciples traveled to the area of Judea and Perea. At one place they stopped, some people began to bring little children to see Jesus. They wanted Him to touch the children. But the disciples didn't think this was a good idea and told the people to go away with their children.

When Jesus saw what was happening, He was furious.

"Let those children come to Me!" He said. "Don't stop them! The kingdom of God belongs to people like them. And I'm going to tell you a very important thing. Anyone who doesn't welcome God's kingdom the way a little child does will never enter it."

Then Jesus put His arms around the children, laid His hands on them and blessed them. ∎

Mark 9:33-37, 42; 10:13-16

Kids

People feel all sorts of ways about kids, Father.
Some people gush all over us.
They say how cute we are
and, my, how we've grown!
That really bugs me.
Other people look at us
as if we'd come from another planet or something.
I think they're afraid we'll bite.
But Jesus really understood kids, didn't He?
He knew we were people who wanted to be near Him
just as the grown-ups did.
He could tell we loved Him
and He said Your kingdom belongs to people like us.
That's great, Father!
We've got a Friend!

The Blind Man

While Jesus was walking in Jerusalem one day, He saw a man who had been blind all his life.

"Teacher," said His disciples, "who did the bad thing. Was it this man or his parents? Why did God make him blind?"

"He didn't do anything wrong and neither did his parents," said Jesus. "He was born blind so that God's power might be seen through him."

Then Jesus spit on the ground, made a little paste, and put it on the blind man's eyes.

"Go wash yourself in the Pool of Siloam," He said to the man.

The man did this and then he could see.

Some people in the neighborhood saw him and said to one another, "Isn't that the man who used to sit and beg?"

"Yes," said some.

"No, he just looks like that man," said others.

"I am the man," said the man Jesus had cured.

"Well, how is it that you can see now?" asked the people.

The man told them what Jesus had done for him.

"Where is this Jesus?" asked the people.

"I don't know," said the man.

The people took the man to the church leaders, and he told them too what Jesus had done.

"This Jesus cannot come from God," said the church leaders. "He healed this man on the Sabbath and no one from God would do that. What do you think about Him?"

"I think He is a prophet," said the man.

"You know," said one of the church leaders, "I'm not so sure that this man was ever blind. I think we'd better ask his parents."

So they sent for the man's parents.

"Has your son really been blind since he was born?" asked the church leaders.

"Yes," they said.

"Well, how come he can see now?" asked the church leaders.

"You'll have to ask him that," said the man's parents. "He's old enough to speak for himself." They were afraid of the church leaders and their questions.

So the church leaders sent for the man again.

"We know that this Jesus is a sinner," they said to him.

"I don't know if He is or not," said the man. "All I know is that I used to be blind and now I can see."

"How did He do that for you?" asked the leaders.

"I already told you once and you wouldn't listen," said the man. "Why do you want to

hear it again? Do you want to become His disciples?"

"We certainly do not!" said the church leaders. "You can be His disciple. *We* are disciples of Moses. We know that God spoke to Moses. But we don't even know where this Jesus comes from."

"This is really strange," said the man. "We know that He made me see. He wouldn't have been able to do that if He didn't come from God."

"Are you trying to teach us, you sinner?" yelled the leaders. And they drove the man away.

Jesus heard what had happened and found the man.

"Do you believe in the Son of Man?" He asked him.

"Tell me who He is, Sir," said the man, "so that I can believe in Him."

"You are looking at Him and He is speaking to you," said Jesus.

"'Lord, I believe," said the man.

"I have come into the world," said Jesus, "so that those who do not have sight may see and those who do have sight may not see."

"Surely *we* can see," said some church leaders who were standing nearby.

"If you couldn't see, you wouldn't be guilty," said Jesus. "But since you say that you are able to see, you are judged guilty of the wrong things you do." ■

John 9

Prayer

I would not like to be blind, Father.
I'm glad Jesus healed some people who were.
I wonder if He did that
because He loved those people
and wanted to show them
how beautiful Your world really is.
Or did He do it for another reason too?
Did He do it to show everyone Your love,
to show them the way You want
the world to be
—no sickness, no sadness, no pain?
I can't work any miracles, Father.
But please help me show Your love
in whatever ways I can
by trying to make this world
a better place.

Amen.

The Good Shepherd

Then Jesus told the church leaders a story about sheep.

"The only people who sneak into a sheepfold are thieves and robbers," He said. "The shepherd of the flock goes in through the gate. The gatekeeper lets him in. Then the shepherd calls to his own sheep. They recognize his voice and follow him out of the sheepfold. He walks along and leads them and they follow him because they know his voice. But they run away from a stranger because they do not know his voice."

But the people did not understand this story, so Jesus talked to them some more.

"I am the gate of the sheepfold," He said. "All the others have been thieves and robbers and the sheep haven't paid any attention to them. But I am the gate and whoever comes in through Me will be safe. Thieves come to kill and destroy, but I have come to give life.

"I am the Good Shepherd. The Good Shepherd will die for his sheep. A hired man won't do that. He isn't the shepherd and the sheep do not belong to him. When he sees a wolf coming, he runs away. Then the wolf attacks the sheep.

"But I am the Good Shepherd. I know My sheep and My sheep know Me. I wil give up My life for My sheep. And I have other sheep too—ones that aren't in this sheepfold. I have to lead them too and they will follow My voice. One day there will be just one flock and one Shepherd.

"My Father loves me because I will give up My life. No one will take it from Me. I will give it up of My own free will. I have the power to give it up. And I have the power to begin it again."

The church leaders got really upset by what Jesus had said. "He is crazy!" some of them said. "Don't even bother to listen to Him!"

Others said, "No, these are not the words of a crazy man. Could a crazy man make a blind person see?" ■

John 10:1-21

Prayer

Who am I in that story Jesus told?
Am I one of the sheep
that Jesus gave up His life for?
I guess I am.
But sometimes I am the other things too.
Sometimes I am a wolf and hurt others.
Sometimes I am a hired man and run away.
And sometimes I am a shepherd.
I try to care for others
and keep them safe.
Father, thank You for making me
one of Jesus' sheep.

Forgive me for the times
when I am a wolf or a hired man.
And help me be a shepherd to others
so that everyone will someday be
part of Your Son's flock.

Amen.

The Disciples Are Sent Out

After a while, Jesus appointed 70 more disciples and sent them out into the world in pairs. They were to go to all the places He would visit later.

"The harvest is rich," He said to them, "but there aren't many workers. Ask God to send workers to His harvest. Remember, too, that I am sending you out like lambs among wolves. Don't carry anything with you. Don't greet anyone on the road. When you go into a house, say first of all, 'Peace be to this house.' If the people there are peaceful, your peace will rest on them. If they aren't, your peace will come back to you.

"When you go into friendly towns, tell the people that God's kingdom is very near to them. If a town is unfriendly, shake its dust off your feet. But tell those people too that God's kingdom is very near them. Anyone who listens to you is listening to Me."

When the 70 disciples came back to Jesus, they were filled with joy.

"Lord," they said, "even the devils listen to us when we use Your name."

"Yes," said Jesus, "I have given you that power. But don't let it make you joyful. Instead, be joyful that your names are written in heaven. Happy are the eyes that see what

you see. Many prophets and kings wanted to see these things and couldn't. Many of them wanted to hear what you have heard, but they couldn't." ■

Luke 10:1-24

Prayer

What a trip those disciples took, Father!
How scary it must have been,
setting out with nothing,
and how neat to discover the power
Jesus had given them.

But power wasn't the important thing,
was it, Father?
The important thing was that those disciples
knew Jesus and all He taught about You.
The power was just to help them
teach others about Him.
Well, I'm ready to make that trip too.
Please give me the power that I'll need.
But even more
give me the important thing.
Give me the eyes to see Jesus,
the ears to hear Him,
and the heart to follow Him.

Amen.

The Good Samaritan

One day a lawyer decided to try to trick Jesus. "Teacher," he said, "what must I do to have eternal life."

"What do you read in the Law?" asked Jesus.

"'You must love the Lord with all your heart, with all your soul, and with all your strength,'" he quoted. "'And you must love your neighbor as yourself.'"

"That's right," said Jesus. "If you do those things, eternal life is yours."

"And who is my neighbor?" asked the man. Then Jesus told this story:

"Once a man was on his way from Jerusalem to Jericho. Robbers got hold of him. They took everything he had, beat him, and ran away, leaving him half dead.

"Now a priest happened to be traveling along the road, but when he saw the man, he just walked by on the other side. A church official did the same thing. Then a traveler from Samaria came along. When he saw the poor man, he went over to him and bandaged his wounds. He poured oil and wine on them

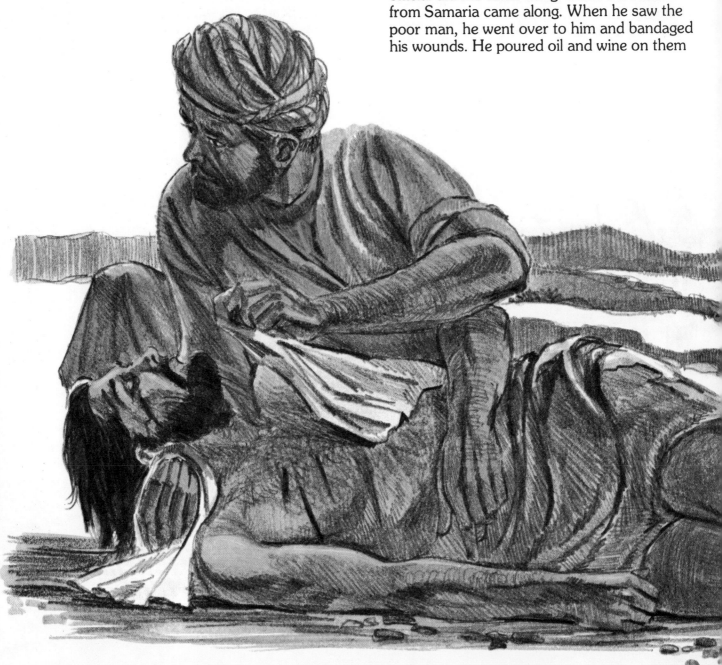

to make them feel better. Then he lifted him onto his own donkey and took him to an inn. There he took care of him for the rest of the day. The next day he gave the innkeeper some money and told him to look after the man till he came back.

"'I'll pay for anything that man needs,' said the Samaritan.

"Now," said Jesus, "which of those three people who came along the road acted like the poor man's neighbor?"

"The one who took care of him," said the lawyer.

"Go and do the same thing yourself," said Jesus. ∎

Luke 10:25-37

Prayer

That story about the Good Samaritan makes me think of a lot of questions, Father.
Who can I be a neighbor to?
The kid at school that nobody likes?
The bully that everyone's scared of?
Some poor kid in my community?
Some poor kid in another country?
I guess they all need a good neighbor
and I guess if I really thought,
I could figure out some way
to be that neighbor.
But I'm only one person, Father.
I can't do everything myself.
Help me decide which people need me most
and send others
to be good neighbors to the rest.

Amen.

Mary and Martha

While Jesus and His disciples were traveling, they came to a village where a woman called Martha and her sister Mary lived.

"Welcome, Lord," said Martha when she saw Him. "Come into my house."

So Jesus went in, and right away Mary sat down at His feet to listen to Him teach.

But Martha didn't have time to do that. She was worried about making Jesus comfortable and getting Him something to eat.

"Lord, my sister is leaving me to do all the work myself," she grumbled. "Don't you care about that? Please tell her she should be helping me."

"Martha, Martha," said Jesus. "You worry and fuss about so many things. But few things are needed. In fact, only one thing is needed. Mary has chosen the better part. It will not be taken away from her." ■

Luke 10:38-42

Prayer

Poor old Martha!
I know a bunch of people like her.
They spend all their time worrying
about whether they're doing the right thing
or not
and whether everyone else is too.
They fuss about food and they
fuss about clothes
and they fuss about a speck of dust
on the rug.
They fuss so much that they
make you uncomfortable
even while they think they're
making you comfortable.

Sure, it's important to eat good food
and wear proper clothes
and live in a clean house.
But none of those things is
as important as Jesus
and what He has to say.
Father, help me to know
the right thing to do
at the right time.
Help me choose the better part,
as Mary did.
Help me choose Jesus.

Amen.

Talking to God

One time Jesus was praying, and when He'd finished, one of His disciples asked Him to teach them how to pray too.

"This is what you should say," said Jesus.

"Our Father, who art in heaven,
hallowed be Thy name.
Thy kingdom come.
Thy will be done on earth
as it is in heaven.
Give us this day our daily bread
and forgive us our trespasses
as we forgive those
who trespass against us.
And lead us not into temptation,
but deliver us from evil.
For Thine is the kingdom
and the power and the glory,
forever and ever. Amen."

Then Jesus told His disciples a story. "What if you went to see a friend of yours in the middle of the night. You wake him up and say, 'My friend, please lend me three loaves of bread. Another friend of mine has just arrived at my house and I don't have any food to give him.' Your friend answers from inside his house, 'Don't bother me! I've already locked the door and my whole family is in bed. I can't get up and give you any bread.'

"Now," said Jesus, "maybe that friend won't give you the bread just because he is your friend. But if you bother him long enough, he'll give it to you just to get rid of you.

"God cares much more about you than some friend you wake up in the middle of the night. Ask Him for what you need and He will give it to you. Search for what you want and you will find it. Knock on the door and it will be opened for you. If you were a father and your son asked you for some bread, would you give him a stone instead? If he asked you for a fish, would you give him a snake? If he asked you for an egg, would you give him a scorpion? You are evil people, but you know how to give your children good things. Just think how much more God will give you!"

Luke 11:1-13

Just Words

The prayer Jesus taught us is beautiful, Father.
I know it is the best prayer there is.
But sometimes I say it so often,
that I forget to think about it.
I say just words
and then I feel guilty
and not close to You at all.
Maybe I need to talk to You
about *why* I can't concentrate.
Maybe I need to tell You
about the things that are really on my mind
when I'm trying to pray.
Then, after we get through all that stuff,
maybe I'll be able to pray
the prayer Jesus taught
with all my heart.

The Silly Rich Man

One day Jesus was teaching a crowd of people when a man spoke up.

"Teacher," he said, "my father died and left some money to my brother and me, and my brother won't give me any of it. Tell him he has to do that."

"My friend," said Jesus, "who said that I am the person to handle your arguments? Be careful, all of you, of being greedy. Your life isn't made safe by what you own—even if you own a lot.

Then Jesus told this story. "Once there was a rich man who had an especially good harvest one year. 'Well, well,' he said to himself. 'What am I going to do? I don't have enough room to store all my crops. I know! I'll take down my barns and build bigger ones. I'll put everything I own in them. Then I'll eat and drink and have a very good time because I have everything I need for years and years.'

"But God said to this rich man, 'You silly fellow! This very night you are going to die and what good will all those things you own do you then?' That's the way it is when people depend on the things they own.

"And that's why I'm telling you not to worry about your life or what you eat or your body or what you wear. Life means more than food and the body means more than clothes. Think about the birds. They don't plant seeds or gather harvests. They don't have any barns. But God feeds them. And you are worth a lot more to God than the birds are!

"Think about the flowers. They don't spin and weave cloth. But not even Solomon was dressed as beautifully as they are. And you are worth much more to God than the flowers.

"Don't worry about *things*! God knows you need them. You put His kingdom first in your lives and He'll take care of the rest. There is no reason for you to be afraid." ■

Luke 12:13-32

Prayer

I like that story, Father,
especially the part about the birds and
flowers.
I can just see a bird driving a little
tractor
or a flower running a tiny sewing machine.
It's so silly!
But I guess that's how we look to You
when we get all hung up about *things*,
when we worry about hamburgers
or tennis shoes
or new bikes.
Why, You made this whole world,
including us.
You've promised to love and care for us.
I guess You can take care of hamburgers
and tennis shoes and bikes!
Help me understand that, Father,
deep inside.
Help me stop being so silly!

Amen.

Dinner Stories

One Sabbath Day Jesus went to dinner at the home of an important church leader. Everyone watched Him carefully to see what He would do. Suddenly a sick man stood before Him.

"Now," said Jesus to all the church leaders, "is it against the law to make a sick person well on the Sabbath or not?"

The church leaders wouldn't say a word.

So Jesus made the sick man well and sent him home. Then He turned back to the leaders. "If your son fell into a well on the Sabbath," He said, "would you pull him out? If your ox fell into a well on the Sabbath, would you pull it out?"

The leaders couldn't think of any answer to these questions.

Now Jesus had noticed how they all rushed to sit in the best places at the dinner table.

"When someone asks you to a wedding party," He said, "don't sit in the best place. Maybe your host has saved that place for a more important person. Then he'd have to tell you to move, and wouldn't you be embarrassed? No, when you go to someone's house, sit in the worst place. Then your host will be able to tell you to sit someplace better, and everyone will know that you are his special friend. People who make themselves important will be put down. But people who don't make themselves important will be lifted up.

"And when you give a party, don't just ask the people that you know will ask you back to their parties. Ask the people that can't afford to give parties themselves. God will reward you."

"How happy the people will be who will feast in God's kingdom!" said someone at the table.

"Well," said Jesus, "this is how it is. Once a man gave a great party and invited many people. When everything was ready, he sent out his servant to get the people he'd invited. But they all started to make excuses. 'I can't come,' said one of them. 'I just bought a piece of land and I have to go look at it.' 'I can't come," said another. 'I just bought some oxen and I have to go try them out.' ' I can't come,' said a third one. 'I just got married.'

"The servant came back and told his master about all these excuses. The man was furious. 'All right,' he said. 'Go out into the streets and alleys and bring in all the poor people you can find.' The servant did this and there was still room left at the table. 'Fine,' said the man. 'Go out on the highways and find people there. I want my house to be full for this party!'

"You see," said Jesus. "that's the way it is in God's kingdom too. Some people just won't come." ■

Luke 14:1-24

The Party

Why wouldn't they, Father?
Why wouldn't people come
to the wonderful party
in Your kingdom?
Didn't they know what they were missing?
I guess they didn't.
I guess they thought fields and oxen
and getting married were more important.
It's back to that "What's important?"
question again,
isn't it?
But the poor people knew.
They didn't have any *things*,
so *things* couldn't get in their way.
I don't want to be poor, Father,
and I don't want anyone else
to be poor either.
But I'd like to be able to act like those
poor people did.
I'd like to forget about things
and come to the party!

Some Lost Things

Now the tax collectors and other people who had done bad things loved to listen to Jesus. They felt as if He were speaking especially to them. But this bothered the church leaders.

"This man welcomes sinners and even eats with them!" they complained.

So Jesus told them some stories about how things are in God's kingdom.

"Suppose you had a hundred sheep," He said, "and one of them got lost. Wouldn't you leave the other 99 alone and go out searching for that lost sheep? And when you found it, wouldn't you lift it up on your shoulders and joyfully carry it home? And when you got home, wouldn't you call your friends and neighbors together and have a party to celebrate?

"I tell you that in God's kingdom there is more joy about one sinner who repents than

there is about 99 good people who don't have to repent."

Then Jesus told another story.

"Once a woman had ten coins and lost one of them. At once she lit the light, swept out the whole house, and looked everywhere until she found it. Then she called together her friends and neighbors and had a party to celebrate. That's the way God's angels feel when one sinner repents." ■

Luke 15:1-10

Prayer

I think I understand what Jesus was saying
in those stories, Father.
I can kind of see how it would be for me
if I had a puppy
and one day she wandered away.
I wouldn't stop to think about the clothes
in my closet
or the bike in the garage
or the food in the refrigerator.
I'd just think about my puppy
and I'd look for her
until I found her.
Then I'd feel like having a party.
I know I would.
So that's the way You feel about people
who want to stop being bad
and start following Jesus.
They're found!
Let's celebrate!

Amen.

The Lost Son

Then Jesus told still another story.

"A man had two sons and one day the younger one said to his father, 'Father, I want the money that you would leave to me.' So the father gave him the money.

"A few days later, the young man packed up all his belongings and went away to another country. There he spent all his money eating rich foods, drinking fine wines, and having fun with other people who liked to spend money.

"Finally, though, his money ran out and, just about that same time, the country where he was staying had a terrible famine. The son had to figure out some way to earn money just to stay alive. So he hired himself out to a farmer who gave him the job of feeding the pigs. The son got so hungry that he wanted to eat the pigs' food himself. But no one offered him any food of his own.

"Then one day he started thinking. 'My father's servants get enough to eat,' he thought, 'and here I am starving to death. I think I'll go home. I'll tell my father that I've sinned against heaven and against him. I'll say that I no longer deserve to be called his son. And I'll ask if I can just be one of his servants.'

"So the son started for home. While he was still a long way off, his father saw him coming. His heart was touched and he ran to meet the boy and hugged him and kissed him.

"'Father,' said the son, 'I have sinned against heaven and against you. I don't deserve to be called your son anymore.'

"But his father called to his servants. 'Quick!' he said. 'Bring out the best robe and put it on my son. Put a ring on his finger and sandals on his feet. Kill a calf and cook it. We're going to have a party! My son was dead and now he is alive again. He was lost, but now he is found.' And they began to have the party.

"Meanwhile, the older son was out working in the fields. As he started home, he could hear the noise of the party in the house. 'What's going on?' he asked one of the servants.

"'Your brother has come home,' said the servant, 'and your father has killed a calf and is having a party because he is safe.'

"This made the older brother angry, and he wouldn't go into the house. Finally his father came out to talk to him.

"'Look,' said the older brother, 'I've worked and slaved for you for years. I've never disobeyed you. But you've never had a party for me. Not even a little one. And here's my brother who's done all sorts of bad things and you kill a calf for his party.'

"'But, my son,' said the father, 'you are always with me and everything I have is yours. It is right that we have a special party for your brother. He was dead and now he is alive. He was lost and now he is found.'" ■

Luke 15:11-32

The Other One

When I think about the story
of the son who left home,
I always pretend that I'm him.
I know that's how You feel about me,
Father.
I know You'll always welcome me back,
no matter how far I go
or what I do.
It feels good to know that, Father.
But maybe sometimes I should pretend
to be the other son,
the one who stayed home.
How would I feel if You welcomed home
someone who had done *terrible* things?
How would I feel if You loved that person
just as much as You love me?
You do it all the time, Father.
How *do* I feel?

Lazarus

Mary and Martha, the two women who had made friends with Jesus, lived in the town of Bethany with their brother Lazarus. One day Lazarus became very ill. Mary and Martha sent a message to Jesus. "Lord, the man You love is ill," it said.

When Jesus got the message, He said, "This illness will not end up in death. It will end up with God's glory and God's Son will be glorified."

Now Jesus really loved Mary, Martha, and Lazarus, but He didn't hurry right off to their town. Instead He stayed where He was for two more days. Then He said to His disciples, "All right. Let's go to Bethany."

"That might not be such a safe thing to do," said the disciples. "Some people there wanted to stone You the last time You went."

But Jesus said He was going anyway. "Our friend Lazarus is resting," He added. "I am going to wake him up."

"If he's resting, Lord, he's sure to get better," said the disciples.

"You don't understand," said Jesus. "Lazarus is dead. And I am glad I was not there to heal him before He died. Maybe now you will believe in Me. But come on! Let's go!"

By the time they got to Bethany, they found out that Lazarus had already been in his tomb for four days. Many people had come to Mary and Martha's house to offer their sympathy. Martha rushed out of the house to greet Jesus, but Mary just sat inside. "If You had been here, Lord," said Martha, "Lazarus would not have died. But I know that even now You can ask God for anything and He will give it to You."

"Your brother will rise again," said Jesus.

"Yes, I know he will do that on the Last Day," said Martha.

"I am the Resurrection," said Jesus. "Anyone who believes in Me will live, even after death. And whoever believes in Me and lives will never die. Do you believe this?"

"Yes, Lord," said Martha. "I believe You are the Christ, the One God sent into the world."

Then she went to call her sister Mary.

"The Master is here," she whispered. "He wants to see you."

Mary got up quickly and hurried to meet Jesus, and the other people who were in the house went with her. As soon as Mary saw Jesus, she threw herself on the ground at His feet.

"If You had been here, Lord," she said, "my brother would not have died." She was crying and so were the people with her.

When Jesus saw her tears, He sighed a deep, painful sigh. "Where have you put Lazarus?" He asked.

"Come and see," said the people.

Then Jesus cried too and the people said, "See how much He loved Lazarus!"

But a few people couldn't stop being nasty even then. "He made that blind man see," they said. "Couldn't He have kept Lazarus from dying?"

Finally Jesus got to the tomb. It was a cave with a rock over the opening.

"Take the rock away," said Jesus.

"Lord, he has been in there four days," said Martha. "He will smell by now."

"Didn't I tell you that if you believe you will see God's glory?" asked Jesus.

So they took the rock away. Then Jesus looked upward and prayed. "Father, thank You for hearing My prayer. I know that You always hear Me, but I want all these people

around Me to know that it was You who sent Me."

Then Jesus cried in a loud voice, "Lazarus, come out of there!"

And Lazarus came out of the tomb. The gravecloths were still wrapped around him.

"Take off those cloths," said Jesus. "Let him go free."

Of course the church leaders found out about what Jesus had done. It scared them that so many people were beginning to believe in Jesus.

"We have to do something about this!" they said.

"Yes," said Caiaphas, one of the leaders. "It is better that He should die."

And from then on they began trying to figure out ways to kill Jesus. ∎

John 11:1-53

Prayer

Martha knew too, Father.
She knew You would give Jesus
anything He asked,
even if He asked You
to make Lazarus alive again.
She knew Jesus was Your Son.
She *believed*.
And You did it, Father.
You made Lazarus alive again.
That's exactly what You'll do
for me someday, isn't it?
Because of Jesus,
You'll make me alive again.
Oh, Father, that's such good news!

Amen.

The 10 Sick People

One day Jesus was traveling along the border between Samaria and Galilee. He came to a village and started to go in when 10 people with leprosy came up to Him. Leprosy is a skin disease and people who had it back then were not allowed near other people. These 10 people wouldn't get too close to Jesus either.

"Jesus, Master!" they called. "Have pity on us!"

"Go show yourselves to the priests," said Jesus. People did this to prove that they didn't have leprosy. And as these people went to visit the priests, they were made well again.

Nine of them kept running to find the priest. But one turned back and began praising God at the top of his voice. He threw himself at Jesus' feet and thanked Him. This man was a Samaritan.

"Didn't I make 10 people well?" asked Jesus. "What happened to the other nine? It looks like the only one who came back to praise God is this man from Samaria. Stand up, then, and go your way. Your faith has saved you." ■

Luke 17:11-19

Prayer

I would have been one of the nine, Father.
I would have forgotten to say "Thank You."
I would have been so excited
about being well,
that thanking Jesus wouldn't even have
occurred to me.
In fact, I guess I'm one of the nine
every day.
There are so many things to thank You for
and most of the time I don't even bother.
I guess I never stopped to think that
it might be important to You.
Well, I guess it's time to change the score
from 9-1 to 8-2.
Thanks, Father!
Thanks for everything!

Amen.

The Pharisee and the Publican

One day Jesus was talking to some people who thought they were as good as anyone could possibly be. They looked down on everyone else and thought they were nothings. So Jesus told them this story.

"Two men went to the temple to pray. One was a Pharisee, a church leader. The other was a publican, a tax collector.

"The Pharisee stood there and said this prayer to himself. 'I thank You, God, that I am not greedy, unjust, and evil like everyone else. I thank You especially that I'm not like this tax collector here. Why, I fast twice a week. I give some of everything I get to the church.'

"Meanwhile, the tax collector stood a little distance away and would not even look up to heaven. Instead he beat his breast and said, 'God, be merciful to me, a sinner.'

"This tax collector," said Jesus, "went home forgiven by God, but the Pharisee did not. Everyone who makes himself important will be put down. But people who don't think they are important will be lifted up." ■

Luke 18:9-14

Prayer

When I hear that story, Father,
I think that I'm like the tax collector.
I know I do wrong things.
I'm greedy and lazy.
I don't help poor people enough.
There's a lot wrong with me.
I'm glad I can ask You for mercy
and know that You'll give it.
But do you know what, Father?
There's a tricky bit in that story.
If I'm not careful,
I might just say someday,

"I thank You that I'm not
like that Pharisee."
And that would be the same thing he did!
So I'm going to make my prayer very simple,
Father.
Thank You for forgiving me
—just as I am.

Amen.

The Rich Man

One day Jesus and His disciples were getting ready to leave on another trip. All at once a rich young man ran up, kneeled down before Jesus, and asked Him a question.

"What do I have to do to have eternal life, good Master?" he said.

"Why do you call Me good?" asked Jesus. "Only God is good. And you know what you have to do. You know the commandments. You must not kill. You must not steal. You must not bring false witness. You must not cheat. You must honor your father and mother."

"But, Master," said the rich young man, "I've obeyed all those commandments ever since I was a little child."

Jesus looked right at him, His eyes full of love. "Then there's only one more thing you must do," He said. "Go and sell everything you own and give the money to poor people. Then you will have treasure in heaven. And you must come and follow Me."

A strange, sad look came to the young man's face when Jesus said these things. He had a great deal of money, and he just didn't see how he could give it all away. So he went away from Jesus.

Then Jesus turned to His disciples.

"It is so hard," He said, "for rich people to enter God's kingdom."

"It is?" said the disciples. They were astonished by what He said.

"Yes, it is," said Jesus. "My children, it's easier for a camel to go through the eye of a needle than it is for a rich person to enter God's kingdom."

"But if that's true," said the disciples, "then who can be saved?"

"For people it is impossible," said Jesus. "But for God anything is possible."

"How about us then?" asked Peter. "We have given up everything to follow You."

"Listen," said Jesus. "I am serious. Anyone who has left house, family, land, or anything else for My sake and for the sake of the Good News of God's love will be paid back a

hundred times over. You will be rewarded in this life now and in the world to come too. You see, many of the people who seem to be first now will end up being last. And many of the people who seem to be last now will end up being first." ■

Mark 10:17-31

Prayer

It's hard for a rich person
to enter Your kingdom.
That's what Jesus said, Father.
I can see why His disciples were confused,
until I remember
how different Your kingdom is.
Money doesn't mean much there,
does it, Father?
Neither do things, the stuff we own.
That might be sort of hard
for a rich person to get used to.
I'm glad Jesus added the last part,
the part where He said
everything was possible for You.
Please help the rich people, Father.
I want *everyone* to live in Your kingdom.

Amen.

104

Zacchaeus

Jesus traveled to the town of Jericho and was walking through the city. Now in Jericho there lived a man called Zacchaeus. He was one of the senior tax collectors and he was very rich. He wanted to take a good look at Jesus, but there was a huge crowd and Zacchaeus was too short to see over the heads of the others.

So he ran ahead of the crowd and climbed a sycamore tree. He figured that he'd be able to look down and see Jesus when He came along.

Well, along came Jesus all right, but He didn't go on past the tree. He stopped and looked up.

"Zacchaeus," He said, "come on down. And hurry. I want to stay at your house today."

Zacchaeus leaped down from the tree and said to Jesus, "Oh, Master, you will be very

welcome!" So they both went to Zacchaeus' house.

This didn't make some of the other people in the crowd too happy, though.

"Jesus has gone to stay with a sinner?" they said.

But something had happened to Zacchaeus. "Lord," he said, "I am going to give half of what I own to the poor. If I have cheated anyone, I will pay that person back four times over."

"Salvation has come to this house today, Zacchaeus," said Jesus. "I have come to find those who were lost." ■

Luke 19:1-10

Prayer

Everyone knew Zacchaeus was a bad man.
So they treated him like a bad man.
And so he went on being a bad man.
It was like a big trap
and Zacchaeus couldn't get out.
Not until Jesus came.
He didn't treat Zacchaeus like a bad man.
He treated him like a friend.
And then the trap sprang open.
Zacchaeus jumped out
and started acting like Jesus' friend.
Father, thank You for sending Jesus.
Thank You for opening the traps
for people like Zacchaeus
and me.
Help me open traps for others.
Help me treat them like Your children.

Amen.

Palm Sunday

Then the time came for Jesus to go to Jerusalem and celebrate the Passover with His disciples. When they were near the city, Jesus sent two of His disciples ahead to the village of Bethphage.

"In the village you will find a donkey and her colt. Untie them and bring them to Me. If anyone says anything to you, tell them, 'The Master needs them. He will send them back soon.'"

The two disciples hurried off to the village and brought back the donkey and her colt. They put their cloaks on the backs of the colt and Jesus sat on it.

Then great crowds of people came and threw their cloaks on the road. Others cut branches from trees and spread them on the ground to make a green carpet. Crowds went in front of Jesus and crowds followed behind Him and all of them were shouting.

"Hosanna to the Son of David!" they cried. "Blessed is He who comes in the name of the Lord. Hosanna in the highest!"

By the time they got to Jerusalem, the whole city was bubbling with shouts and questions.

"Who is this person in the parade?" people asked.

"This is the prophet Jesus from Nazareth," others answered.

The next day Jesus went to the temple. Now people had gotten into the habit of doing business in the temple. They exchanged money from other countries and they sold animals. Jesus was furious when He saw all this. He knocked over the tables of the moneychangers and pushed down the chairs of the animal sellers.

"Scripture says that God's house is a house of prayer," He said. "But you have turned it into a den of thieves!"

Then Jesus cured some blind people and some people who could not walk. Children were in the temple too and they kept shouting, "Hosanna to the Son of David!"

Finally the church leaders couldn't stand it anymore. "Do You hear what those children are saying?" they asked.

"Yes," said Jesus. "And haven't you read in Scripture that God uses children to make sure He is praised?"

Then Jesus left the temple and spent the night in the town of Bethany. ■

Matthew 21:1-17

Prayer

"Hosanna! Hosanna!
Blessed is He that comes in the name
of the Lord!"
They welcomed Him and sang Him praises.
Oh, it was such a day,
a day of triumph and rejoicing.
And then,
a few days later,
they shouted again.
"Crucify Him!" they cried.
"Crucify Him!"
And I was there both times, Father.
I was in both crowds.
I still am.
I sing His praise with all my heart
and then I crucify Him with my sins.
Forgive me, Father.
Forgive us all.

Amen.

108

The Last Supper

When the day came to eat the Passover meal, Jesus sent Peter and John to get ready for it.

"Where shall we have the meal?" they asked Him.

"As you go into the city," said Jesus, "you will see a man carrying a pitcher of water. Follow him and talk to the owner of the house he enters. Tell him that the Master wants to know where the dining room is that He may celebrate the Passover with His disciples. The man will show you a large room with couches. Get ready for the meal there."

And that's exactly what Peter and John did.

Meanwhile, Satan had gotten into Judas, one of the other disciples. He convinced Judas to help the church leaders arrest Jesus. For his help Judas would be paid 30 pieces of silver.

Jesus knew all of this; He knew that His work on earth was nearly complete. But before He went back to His Father, He wanted to show His disciples what love was really like. So He got up from the dinner table, took off His cloak, and wrapped a towel around His waist. Then He poured some water into a basin and began to wash His disciples' feet.

When He got to Peter, Peter said, "Lord, are You going to wash my feet?"

"You don't know exactly what I'm doing now, Peter," said Jesus. "But you will understand later."

"I will never let You wash my feet, Lord!" said Peter

"If you don't let Me wash your feet, I can't be a part of you," said Jesus.

"Then wash my hands and head too!" said Peter.

After Jesus had finished washing His disciples' feet, He went back to the table and sat down. "Do you understand what I have done?" He asked. "You call me Master and Lord and you are right. But if your Master and Lord has washed your feet, then you should wash each other's feet too. No servant is greater than the master. I have showed you what to do so that you will copy Me."

Then they began to eat and Jesus said, "I have wanted so much to eat this meal with you. I will not eat it again until the kingdom of God has completely come."

He took a cup of wine, gave thanks to God, and said, "Take this wine and share it. I shall not drink this wine again until the kingdom of God completely comes."

Then He took some bread, gave thanks to God, broke it, and gave it to His disciples. "This is My body, which will be given for you," He said. "Do this to remember Me."

After supper He took the wine again and said, "This cup is My blood of the New Covenant, which will be poured out for you.

"And here on the table," continued Jesus, "is the hand of the man who will betray Me. Alas for him!"

At once everyone began asking everyone else who that might be.

A little later Jesus turned to Peter. "I have prayed that your faith will not fail," He said. "Once you have recovered, you will have to give strength to the others."

"Lord, I will go to prison with You," said Peter. "I would even die with You!"

"Peter," said Jesus, "by the time the rooster crows, you will have said three times that you don't even know Me." ∎

John 13:1-20
Luke 22:1-34

His Supper

It is a mystery beyond my understanding,
Father.
He said the bread was His body
and the wine was His blood.
He told us to eat and drink
and somehow, in some way, He would
be with us.
I don't understand, Father.
But maybe my understanding isn't
so important.
After all, it is Your Son's gift to us,
this mystery, this feast.
He makes it happen
and invites us to be there.
Isn't that the important thing,
that He wants me at His supper?
I guess I'll leave the rest of it to Him,
Father.
I'll just come—and celebrate!

Jesus' Arrest and Trial

After the meal, Jesus left the house and went to the Mount of Olives. His disciples followed Him. When they got there, Jesus went off a little distance to be by Himself and pray.

At last He got up and went back to His disciples. They were so full of grief for Him that they had fallen asleep.

"Why are you asleep?" He asked them. "Get up and pray that you will not be tested."

Jesus was still talking to His disciples when a group of men appeared. In front of them came the disciple Judas. He marched right up to Jesus and started to kiss Him.

"Judas, are you betraying Me with a kiss?" asked Jesus.

"Shall we use our swords, Master?" asked Jesus' disciples. Peter reached for his sword and cut off the right ear of the high priest's servant.

"Stop!" said Jesus. "That will do!" And He made the man's ear well again.

Then Jesus talked to the church leaders who had come to arrest Him. "Am I a robber?" He asked. "Why did you have to come after Me with swords and clubs. Well, this is the hour when darkness is king."

They grabbed Jesus then and led Him away to the high priest's house. Peter followed along behind at a distance. When they got to the house, Peter waited in the courtyard where someone had built a bonfire. A servant girl saw him there.

"This man was with Jesus," she said.

"I was not!" said Peter. "I don't even know Him."

Later someone else saw Peter and said, "You are one of Jesus' followers."

"I am not," said Peter.

An hour passed and then another man said, "This fellow certainly is one of Jesus' followers. He comes from Galilee."

"I don't know what you're talking about!" said Peter.

At that very moment, a rooster crowed. Jesus came into the courtyard and looked right at Peter. And Peter remembered what Jesus had said. He went outside then and wept bitterly.

When daylight came, the Council of Elders had a meeting and Jesus was brought before them.

"If You are the Messiah," they said, "tell us."

"If I tell you, you won't believe Me," said Jesus. "But from now on the Son of Man will be at God's right hand."

"Oh, so You are the Son of God then," they said.

"You have said it," said Jesus.

"We don't need any witnesses," said the council. "He has spoken blasphemy with His own lips."

Next they took Him to Pontius Pilate, the Roman governor.

"This Man has been leading the people to revolt," said the council.

"I can't find anything wrong with Him," Pilate said to the church leaders.

But they kept insisting that Jesus was a troublemaker. Finally they mentioned the fact that He came from Galilee. Pilate breathed a sigh of relief.

"Oh," he said. "In that case, He should be tried by Herod, not me."

So the people took Jesus to see Herod. Herod was delighted. He had heard about Jesus and had been wanting to meet Him for a long time. He hoped Jesus would work a miracle in front of him. So he asked Jesus many questions, but Jesus wouldn't answer any of them. Finally Herod began making fun of Jesus too. He put a fine robe on Him and sent Him back to Pilate.

"Now look," said Pilate. "I haven't been able to find anything wrong with this Man and neither has Herod. So I am going to have Him beaten and then let Him go."

"No!" wailed the people. "Crucify Him! Crucify Him!"

"Why?" asked Pilate. "What has He done?" But the people just yelled louder.

So at last Pilate gave in and handed Jesus over to them. ■

Luke 22:39—23:25

fall asleep when He needed them,
say they never knew Him,
run away and hide?
Could I do those things, Father?
Do I?
Do I betray Him whenever I do wrong?
Do I fill my mind with so many other things
that I cannot hear His voice?
Do I keep quiet sometimes when I should speak up,
because I am embarrassed or scared
to admit that I follow Him?
Do I ever try to take the easy way out
and hide from a hard situation?
Oh, Father, I do!

Betrayal

How could they do it, Father?
How could they betray Him
—Jesus, Your Son?
How could they sell Him to His enemies,

The Crucifixion

They led Jesus away to be crucified, and on the way they met a man called Simon, who was from the land of Cyrene. They made him carry Jesus' cross and walk behind Him. Large numbers of people also followed Jesus, including some women who were crying.

"Don't cry for Me," said Jesus to them. "Cry for yourselves instead."

At last they reached a place called Golgatha, a low hill outside Jerusalem. There they nailed Jesus to the cross. Two criminals were being crucified with Him, one on the right side and one on the left.

Jesus looked at the people who were killing Him and said, "Father, forgive them. They don't know what they are doing."

Then the soldiers played a game to see who would get Jesus' clothing, and in spite of everything that had been done to Jesus, the church leaders still tormented Him.

"He saved others," they joked. "Now let's see Him save Himself."

"If You really are the King of the Jews, save Yourself," said one of the soldiers. Pilate had put a sign on Jesus' cross that said, "This is the King of the Jews."

Even one of the criminals who was being crucified with Jesus made fun of Him. "Aren't You the Messiah?" he asked. Save Yourself then and us too."

"Don't you have any fear of God?" asked the other criminal. "We are suffering the same punishment He is. But we did something to deserve it. He has done nothing wrong. Jesus, remember me when You come into Your kingdom."

"I promise you," said Jesus, "that today you will be with Me in paradise."

At about the sixth hour (noon), darkness covered the earth and stayed until the ninth hour (three o'clock). Then the veil in the temple was torn right down the middle.

Jesus cried out in a loud voice. "Father, into Your hands I give My spirit." Then He died.

The head soldier, who had been there all along, praised God and said, "Surely this was a great and good man."

The people who had just come to watch beat their breasts and went home. And Jesus' friends stood at a distance and watched too.

Then a good man called Joseph of Arimathea came along. He was a member of the council, but he had not agreed with the others. Joseph talked to Pilate and asked if he could have Jesus' body. Pilate agreed and Joseph took Jesus' body off the cross, wrapped it in a gravecloth, and put it in a burial cave where no one had ever been buried before. Then he rolled a stone in front of the cave's opening.

The women who followed Jesus watched all this. They paid careful attention to the exact location of the cave. Then they went home and prepared salves and spices to put on Jesus' body. The next day was the Sabbath and they would have to rest. But on Sunday they would be back. ■

Luke 23:26-56

The Answer

I don't know what to say.
We killed Him, Father.
We killed Your Son,
Your gift of love.
We let Him die alone in agony.
Alone, Father.
Where were You?
Why didn't You stop us?
Father, were You there?
Did You suffer with Him?
Was that part of the plan?
Can Your love for us be as huge as that?
I know the answer, Father.
But I don't know what to say.

Easter

On Sunday, as soon as dawn had broken, the women hurried back to the burial cave with the salves and spices they had prepared. When they got there, they saw that the stone had been rolled away, so they went in. But Jesus' body was not there.

The women just stood there and didn't know what to think. Then, all at once, two men in brilliant clothes were standing beside them. The women were terrified.

"Why are you looking among dead people for someone who is alive?" asked the men. "Jesus is not here. He has risen. Remember all He said to you when you were in Galilee with Him? He said the Son of Man had to be crucified. But He also said that He would rise on the third day."

Then the women remembered and rushed back to tell the others what had happened. Mary Magdalene, Joanna, and Mary, James' mother were in this group. They had followed Jesus for a long time. But when they told their story to the other disciples, no one would believe them.

Then Peter ran out to the tomb to see for himself what was happening. When he got there, he found the gravecloth Jesus had worn, but nothing else. So he went back home too, shaking his head in amazement.

On that same day, two of Jesus' disciples were traveling to a town called Emmaus, which was seven miles from Jerusalem. They were talking together about all that had happened and feeling sad.

Suddenly Jesus began walking along with them, but they were not able to recognize Him. "What are you talking about?" He asked.

The men stopped. "You must be the only person staying in Jerusalem who has not heard," said one of the men whose name was Cleopas.

"Heard about what?" asked Jesus.

So they told Him all about the arrest and death of Jesus and the empty cave the women had found.

"Don't you believe what the prophets said?" asked Jesus. And He began to teach them everything the prophets had said about Him. They finally got to Emmaus and Jesus acted as if He were going on, but the two men urged Him to stay with them.

"It's nearly evening," they said. "The day is almost over."

So Jesus went with them and sat down to a meal. He picked up some bread, gave thanks to God for it, broke it, and gave it to them. Then they knew who He was, but at that moment He vanished.

The men jumped up from the table and rushed back to Jerusalem to tell the others what had happened. They were all still talking about it when suddenly Jesus Himself stood with them.

"Peace be with you!" He said.

They were all terrified; they thought they were seeing a ghost.

"Why are you so upset?" asked Jesus. "Look at My hands and feet. It is really I. Touch Me and see. A ghost doesn't have flesh and bones."

Then they were filled with such great joy that they couldn't say a word, so finally Jesus talked to them again.

"Do you have anything to eat here?" He asked

They gave Him some fish and He ate it.

Now Thomas wasn't with the other disciples when this happened, and he simply couldn't believe what they told him.

"Unless I can see and feel the holes the nails made," he said, "I won't believe any of this."

Eight days later the disciples were all together again, and this time Thomas was there too. All the doors were closed, but suddenly Jesus was standing with them again.

"Peace be with you," He said. "Here, Thomas. Here are My hands. Touch Me and believe."

"My Lord and my God!" said Thomas.

"You believe because you can see Me," said Jesus. "But happy are those people who have not seen Me and still believe in Me." ■

Luke 24:1-43
John 20:24-29

Prayer

It is the day of victory,
the day when everything
is turned upside down.
Death has died and we shall not.
Christ is risen and death has died.
As You breathed into Adam
who brought us death,
so You breathed into Christ
who brings us life.
And our hope is sure:
You will breathe again
and we shall live forever and ever.
Alleluia, Father,
to You and to the Son!
Alleluia! Alleluia!

Amen.

Peter's New Job

One day Jesus' disciples were by the Sea of Galilee.

"I'm going fishing," said Peter.

"We'll come with you," said some of the others.

So they all got into the boat, but they didn't catch anything all night long.

Then daylight came and there stood Jesus on the shore. The disciples didn't realize who He was, though.

"Have you caught anything?" He called.

"No," they answered.

"Throw your net out to the right," He said. "Then you'll find something."

So they did and at once the net was so full of fish that they couldn't lift it into the boat.

"Peter, it is the Lord!" said John.

Peter leaped up, jumped into the water, and hurried to the shore. The other disciples followed him in the boat. When they all got to the shore, they found that Jesus had made a little fire from charcoal and was cooking fish and bread over it.

"Bring some of your fish," Jesus said.

Peter dragged the net up onto the shore and there were 153 big fish in it.

"Come, have breakfast with Me," said Jesus.

Then, after the meal, He turned to Peter.

"Peter, do you love Me more than the others do?" He asked.

"Yes, Lord, You know I love You," said Peter.

"Feed My lambs," said Jesus.

Then Jesus said it again. "Peter, do you love Me?"

"Yes, Lord," said Peter. "You know I love You."

"Feed My sheep," said Jesus.

Then Jesus asked Peter the same question again. "Peter, do you love Me?" Jesus did this to remind Peter of the night he denied his Lord and to assure hm that He still loved him.

This upset Peter. "Lord, You know everything," he said. "You know that I love You."

"Feed My sheep," said Jesus. Then He told Peter how he would someday die, and finally He said, "Follow Me." ■

John 21:1-19

Prayer

I like Peter, Father.
He reminds me of me.
He's always putting his foot in his mouth
or doing the wrong thing.
But he keeps on trying
and he really loves Jesus.
You took old bumbling Peter, Father,
and sent Your Spirit to him.
Your Spirit helped Peter start the church
and it's still going strong!
Your Spirit will help me too, I know.
So use old bumbling me.

Amen.

The Ascension

Jesus showed Himself to His disciples many times for 40 days after God raised Him from death. He talked with them and taught them still more about God's kingdom.

One day He told them to stay in Jerusalem for a while and wait for what the Father had promised to send them.

"It is what I have told you about," He said. "John baptized people with water, but soon you will be baptized with the Holy Spirit."

Then Jesus took His disciples just outside Jerusalem to the edge of Bethany.

"Lord, are You going to restore the kingdom to Israel?" they asked Him. They still thought that Jesus might be going to do something about an earthly kingdom.

"It is not for you to know the times and dates the Father has decided on," He told them. "But you will receive power when the Holy Spirit comes. Then you will tell about Me, not only in Jerusalem, but throughout Judea and Samaria, and even to the ends of the earth."

And as Jesus said this, He was lifted up and a cloud covered Him from their sight. They stood there, staring into the sky, until they noticed two men in white standing with them.

"Why are you looking up into the sky, men from Galilee?" asked the two men. "Jesus has been taken up from you into heaven. But He will come back the same way as you have seen Him go."

And so the disciples went back to Jerusalem to wait for what Jesus had promised. ■

Acts 1:2-12

A Job to Do

I could think about Jesus' going to heaven
for a long time, Father.
I could try to figure out
where heaven is
and what it's like.
But that would be like the disciples'
looking up into the sky.
The two men in white told them
Jesus would come back.
I think they wanted to help
the disciples feel better.
But I think they also meant,
"Get busy!
There's a lot of work to be done
before Jesus comes back."
There sure is, Father.
I'd better get busy too!

Pentecost

When the festival day of Pentecost came around, Jesus' disciples were all together in one room. Suddenly they heard a sound that was like a powerful wind from heaven. Its noise was so great that it filled the whole house. Then they saw something that looked like little tongues of fire. These came apart and rested on the head of each of them. At once the disciples were filled with the Holy Spirit and began to speak foreign languages. This was a gift the Spirit had given them.

Other people in Jerusalem heard the noise and rushed to see what was going on. They were confused, because each of them could hear the disciples in his own language.

"Surely these men are Galileans!" they said. "Why can each of us hear them in his own language? We are from many, many different countries, but we can all hear and understand them preaching and telling about the wonders of God."

No one could explain this wonderful thing, but a few men tried.

"Oh, they are just drunk," they said and laughed.

Then Peter stood up and preached a sermon.

"Don't make a mistake," he said. "We are not drunk. What has happened is that God has sent His Spirit to us. Now listen to what I am going to say! Jesus was sent to you by God and you killed Him. But God raised Him to life again and we all know that. Now He has received the Spirit from God and has poured it out on us. Now you can be certain that God has made Jesus Lord and Christ."

The people who heard this sermon felt terrible about what they had done to Jesus.

"What can we do now?" they asked Peter.

"You must repent," said Peter, "and you

must be baptized in Jesus' name. Then you too will receive the Holy Spirit. That promise is for you and your children. It is for people who are far away and for all people whom God will call."

Peter talked to these people for a long time and by the end of the day about 3,000 of them were baptized.

This was the beginning of the Christian church. The people cared for one another and shared everything they had. Each person had as much as was needed. They all followed the teachings of Jesus' disciples, they drank the wine and ate the bread as Jesus had told them to do, and they prayed.

Every day they went to the temple and praised God, but when they broke the bread, they did it in their own homes. Everyone looked up to them.

The disciples did many miracles and other wonderful things. And day after day, God brought more people to join them in the church of His Son, Jesus. ■

Acts 2

Prayer

What a strange, strange thing
the church is, Father!
It's not a building.
It's not an organization.
It's a group of people,
who aren't really very organized at all,
who act in different ways
and worship you in different ways
and sometimes don't even get along very well
with one another.
But there's one thing that ties them
together
and that's Your Son.
He pours out Your Spirit on them
and makes them His body on earth.
I don't pretend to understand that, Father.
But I think it's great.
And I'm glad I'm a part.

Amen.

The Man at the Beautiful Gate

One day Peter and John were going to the temple to pray. As they were walking along, a crippled man was carried past them. Each day his friends would put him down beside the temple entrance called the Beautiful Gate and he would beg there.

When this man saw Peter and John, he begged from them too.

"Look at us," said Peter and John.

The man looked and hoped he would get some money.

"I don't have any silver or gold," said Peter, "but I will give you what I have. In Jesus' name, walk!"

Then Peter helped the man stand up. At once his feet and ankles became strong. He began to walk and to jump and to praise God, and he followed Peter and John right into the temple.

Everyone saw this and knew he used to be crippled. But they couldn't figure out how he had been made well. So they all ran over to Peter and John.

"Why are you so surprised?" asked Peter. "It is Jesus who has made this man well because of our faith. You are the people who helped kill Jesus, but you didn't know what you were doing. Now it is time for you to turn to Him and believe."

Peter and John talked to the people for quite a while and then some church leaders came over and interrupted them. They were angry that Peter and John were teaching about Jesus. So they arrested them. But it was late and they couldn't hold a trial. So they put Peter and John in jail for the night.

In a way the church leaders were too late, though. Many of the people who had heard Peter and John speak already believed in Jesus.

The next day the church leaders held a meeting. They made Peter and John stand in the middle and began asking them questions.

"By whose name did you make that man well?" they asked.

The Holy Spirit helped Peter, and he said, "If you are asking us about that crippled man we helped, I would be glad to tell you how we did it. I would be glad to tell everyone. We did it in the name of Jesus, the Man you crucified and the One God raised from the dead. His is the only name by which we can be saved."

The leaders were amazed at how well both Peter and John spoke. They thought these men were just fishermen from Galilee. And when they saw the man who had been crippled standing there with them, they couldn't think of anything to say at all.

"Go outside," they ordered the prisoners. "We want to have a private discussion."

So Peter and John went outside and the church leaders talked to one another. "What are we going to do with these men?" they asked. "They performed a miracle and everyone knows it. Maybe we'd just better tell them never to do it again."

So they called Peter and John back in and told them not to perform any more miracles in Jesus' name.

"Shall we listen to you or to God?" asked Peter and John. "We can't stop telling about what we have seen and heard."

The church leaders didn't know what else to do, so they let Peter and John go. And all the people praised God for the wonderful thing the two disciples had done. ■

Acts 3:1—4:21

Prayer

How filled with hate those leaders were, Father!
They couldn't even recognize
the beautiful thing

that had happened to the crippled man
because of Your Son.
Their hate made them see
only something ugly.
Their hate didn't hurt the crippled man,
though.
He could walk again.
And it didn't hurt Peter and John.
They had Your Spirit to help them.
Maybe that's how hate is, Father.
Maybe it hurts the people who are hating
most of all.
It closes their eyes and their hearts
to everything that is good and beautiful.
Father, save me from hate!

Amen.

Stephen

The early church grew and grew and all of its members lived happily together. They cared for one another, shared what they had, and told others about Jesus and what He had done. They met together in a place called Solomon's Porch and other people left them alone while they were meeting. But more and more people saw the wonderful things they did and heard what they said. Soon these people wanted to join them and of course the church welcomed them.

After a while, there were so many members that the disciples didn't have time to give out food to all of them and teach about Jesus too. So they suggested that the people choose seven men to be in charge of giving out the food. The people did, and one of the men they chose was Stephen.

Stephen was filled with the power of God's Spirit too, and he too could work miracles.

But some of the people who did not believe in Jesus hated Stephen because he was more wise than they were. They talked some men into saying that Stephen said untrue things about God. Then they had Stephen arrested and brought him before the Council of Elders, the same group that had tried Jesus. The council looked at Stephen and his face looked like that of an angel.

"Is it true," asked the council, "that you tell people that Jesus is going to destroy the temple and change the laws Moses gave us?"

"Listen to me," said Stephen and he preached a great sermon. He made the

council remember all the wonderful things God had done in the past. And he made them remember how many times God's people had turned against Him in the past. "You are just like those people," said Stephen. "You will not pay attention to God's Spirit."

This made the council furious.

Then God filled Stephen with His Holy Spirit. He let Stephen look into heaven and see God's glory and Jesus standing at God's right hand.

"I can see heaven!" cried Stephen. "And I can see Jesus standing at God's right hand!"

"Stop him!" cried the council. "He is speaking lies about God." They clapped their hands over their ears and then they all rushed at him.

"Take him out of the city!" they shouted. "Stone him until he is dead!"

And that is what they did. They took off their coats and laid them down by a young man called Saul. Then they threw stones at Stephen.

"Lord Jesus, receive my spirit!" cried Stephen. Then he kneeled down. "Don't hold this against them, Lord," he said as he died.

And the young man called Saul watched all this and thought it was right that Stephen should die. From that day on, many people began persecuting the young church in Jerusalem and most of the members ran away to other places. Saul became one of the chief persecutors. He went from house to house, arresting men and women for believing in Jesus, and sending them to prison. ■

Acts 4:32-35; 5:12-16; 6:1—8:3

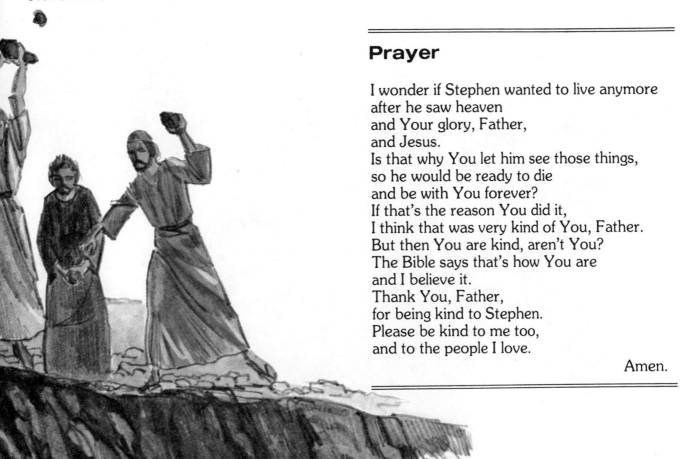

Prayer

I wonder if Stephen wanted to live anymore
after he saw heaven
and Your glory, Father,
and Jesus.
Is that why You let him see those things,
so he would be ready to die
and be with You forever?
If that's the reason You did it,
I think that was very kind of You, Father.
But then You are kind, aren't You?
The Bible says that's how You are
and I believe it.
Thank You, Father,
for being kind to Stephen.
Please be kind to me too,
and to the people I love.

Amen.

Philip and the Ethiopian

One day an angel came to Jesus' disciple Philip and said, "Philip, travel south along the desert road that goes from Jerusalem to Gaza."

Of course Philip obeyed the angel.

Now it happened that there was an Ethiopian, the chief treasurer to the queen of Ethiopia, who had been in Jerusalem and was now traveling home again along that same road. As he drove along in his chariot, he was studying the words the prophet Isaiah had written.

"Go meet that chariot," God's Spirit said to Philip. So Philip did.

"Do you understand what you are reading?" he asked the Ethiopian.

"How can I?" asked the Ethiopian. "I need someone to help me. Here, get into my chariot with me. Maybe you can help me."

So Philip got in and began to explain what Isaiah had written. Soon he was telling the Ethiopian about Jesus too.

After a while, they came to some water.

"Look, there is some water," said the Ethiopian. "Could I be baptized?"

"Of course," said Philip.

The Ethiopian stopped the chariot and the two men went down to the water. Philip baptized the Ethiopian and then suddenly disappeared. The Ethiopian never saw him again. But he was so happy now that he believed in Jesus that he went on home rejoicing.

Philip, meanwhile, found himself in a place called Azotus. So he went on traveling too and told the Good News about Jesus to everyone he met. ■

Acts 8:26-40

Prayer

You sure got Philip where You wanted him
fast, Father.
You gave him his orders
in no uncertain terms.
"Get on that road," said the angel.
"Meet that chariot," said Your Spirit.
Then, whisk!
In a minute You had Philip
somewhere else again,

ready to preach the Good News to more
people.
And I don't think Philip minded a bit.
I don't think I'd mind either,
not as long as I knew the orders
were from You.
So, tell me what to do, Father.
Tell me in no uncertain terms.
Whisk me wherever You want me.
Let's get that Good News told!

Amen.

The Conversion of Saul

Meanwhile, Saul was still persecuting the people who believed in Jesus. He was so anxious to get all of them that he asked the high priest to give him letters that he could take to the city of Damascus. He thought he would find people who believed in Jesus there, arrest them, and take them back to Jerusalem for trial.

As Saul was traveling along the road to Damascus, though, a light from heaven shone all around him. He fell to the ground.

"Saul, Saul," said a voice, "why are you persecuting Me?"

"Who are You, Lord?" asked Saul.

"I am Jesus, the one you are persecuting," said the voice. "Get up now, Saul, and go into the city. You will be told what you have to do."

The men who were traveling with Saul just stood there with their mouths hanging open. They could hear the voice, but they couldn't see anyone.

Saul got up, but he could see nothing. He was blind and the men with him had to lead him into Damascus. For three days Saul was blind, and he wouldn't eat or drink anything.

Meanwhile, a follower of Jesus called Ananias, who lived in Damascus, had a vision. In this vision he heard Jesus saying to him, "Ananias!"

"Here I am, Lord," said Ananias.

"Go to Straight Street," said Jesus, "and ask at the house of Judas for a man called Saul. He is praying right now and he has had a vision of you coming to him and giving him back his sight."

"Lord," said Ananias, "I have heard about this Saul. He has been harming Your people in Jerusalem. And he has come here to harm more people."

"Go to him anyway," said Jesus. "He is the man I have chosen to tell non-Jewish people about Me—and Jewish people too. I will teach him what he needs to know."

So Ananias went at once to the house where Saul was staying and laid his hands on him.

"Brother Saul," he said, "the Lord Jesus has sent me to help you recover your sight and be filled with the Holy Spirit."

At once Saul could see. He asked to be baptized. Then he ate some food and began to grow strong again. ∎

Acts 9:1-19

Amazing

It is absolutely amazing, Father,
that You would pick someone like Saul
for such an important job.
Why, he was an awful person!
He did terrible things to Your people.
I guess it just goes to show
what You can do, Father.
You can take the most awful person,
turn him or her completely around,
and make him or her into one of
Your best servants.
It's amazing, Father.
But it's great too!

The Travels of Peter

Peter traveled around, visiting one place after another, and finally he came to a place called Lydda where some people lived who believed in Jesus. There he met a man called Aeneas, who had been paralyzed for eight years.

"Aeneas, Jesus makes you well!" said Peter. "Get up and fold your mat."

At once Aeneas got up. Everyone who lived in Lydda and in Sharon saw him and they all began to believe in Jesus.

Next Peter went to Jaffa. A woman called Dorcas lived there. She was an extremely good woman and always helped others. But one day she got sick and died. When some of Jesus' followers heard about this, they asked Peter to go to the house where her body was.

The room was filled with people Dorcas had helped, and all of them were crying and showing Peter the clothes Dorcas had made for them.

"Yes, yes," said Peter. "But now you must leave the room." He kneeled down and prayed. Then he turned to Dorcas and said, "Dorcas, stand up!"

Dorcas opened her eyes, looked at Peter, and sat up. Peter helped her stand, and then he called her friends back into the room and showed them that she was alive. Soon everyone in Jaffa heard about this and many of them believed in Jesus too.

Meanwhile, in the city of Caesarea, there lived a Roman officer called Cornelius. Cornelius believed in God but he did not yet believe in Jesus. One day he had a vision in which he saw God's angel come into his house and call out to him.

"Cornelius!"

Cornelius stared at the vision. He was scared. "What is it, Lord?" he asked.

"Your prayers have been answered by God," said the angel. "Send someone to Jaffa and have them bring a man called Peter back to see you."

After the angel had gone, Cornelius sent some of his servants to Jaffa.

While they were still on their way, Peter went up on the roof of the house where he was staying. He was hungry, but his meal wasn't ready yet. While he was up there, he fell into a trance. He saw heaven opening and something that looked like a big sheet being let down to earth by its corners. In the sheet was every kind of animal and bird.

"Kill and eat, Peter," said a voice.

"Oh, no, Lord," said Peter. "I have never eaten anything unclean."

"What God has made clean," said the voice, "you cannot call unclean."

This happened three times, and then the sheet was taken back up into heaven again.

While Peter was trying to figure out what all this meant, Cornelius' servants arrived. Peter was too busy thinking to notice them, so the Holy Spirit spoke to him.

"Some men have come to see you," said the Spirit. "Go back to the place they will take you. I told them to come for you."

Peter went downstairs and told the men who he was. They explained about Cornelius, and the next day Peter went back with them to Caesarea.

Cornelius was waiting for them. He had invited all his relatives and good friends to be with him too. As soon as Peter arrived, Cornelius came out of the house and kneeled in front of him.

"Get up!" said Peter. "I am only a man!"

Then they went into the house and Cornelius introduced Peter to everyone.

"You know," said Peter, "I am a Jew and I am not supposed to mix with non-Jewish people. But God sent me a vision and showed me that it was all right. Why did you send for me, though?"

Cornelius told Peter about the vision he had had.

"I see," said Peter. "And now I understand something that I did not understand before. God does not have favorites. He wants everyone to be His child. Yes, He sent His Son to the Jewish people first. But Jesus is the Lord of all."

Peter went on to tell the people in Cornelius' house more about Jesus. And, as he was talking, God's Spirit came down on everyone there.

"I cannot refuse to baptize all of you," said Peter, "because God has given you His Spirit just as He gave it to me."

So everyone in the house was baptized in Jesus' name. Then they begged Peter to stay with them for a while. ■

Acts 9:32—10:48

Prayer

You don't play favorites, Father.
That's the lesson You taught Peter
and it's a lesson I should remember too.
You didn't send Jesus just for the people
in a particular country
or who belong to a particular church
or behave in a particular way.
You sent Him for everyone.
Everyone!
That's pretty clear, Father.
Help me remember it.

Amen.

Peter in Prison

After a while, King Herod started persecuting the people who believed in Jesus. He cut off the head of Jesus' disciple James and then he decided to arrest Peter too. He put Peter in prison and assigned four teams of guards to take turns watching him. There were four guards on each team. Herod wasn't taking any chances.

All this happened during Passover week and Herod thought he would put Peter on trial at the end of the week. As the days dragged by, the church prayed for Peter day and night.

The night before his trial, Peter was sleeping. He was chained with double chains to two guards, one on either side of Him. Other guards stood at the prison gate.

All at once an angel stood in the cell and it was filled with light. The angel tapped Peter on the side, woke him up, and said, "Get up! Hurry!"

The chains fell off Peter's hands.

"Put on your belt and your sandals," said the angel. "Now put on your cloak and follow me."

Peter followed the angel, but he really didn't believe what was happening. He thought he was having a dream.

The angel led Peter right out of the prison and up to the iron gate that led to the city. This gate opened all by itself and Peter and the angel went through. They walked for another block and then the angel left. That's when Peter caught on.

"This is really happening!" he said. "God really did send His angel to save me from Herod."

He hurried to the house of some church people and knocked at the door. A little servant called Rhoda heard the knocking and went to see who it was. She recognized Peter's voice and was so happy that she ran back into the main room and left Peter standing there.

In the main room were many church people, all praying for Peter.

"He's here! Peter is here!" cried Rhoda.

"You're crazy," said the people.

"No, no, it's true!" said Rhoda.

"Then it must be Peter's ghost," said the people.

Meanwhile, poor Peter was still knocking, and finally the people went and opened the door themselves. When they saw Peter, they were amazed.

Peter waved his hand to make them be quiet. Then he told them what had happened to him. "Tell the others," he said. Then he left and went to another place.

When daylight came, things really got wild at the prison. No one could figure out what had happened to Peter. Herod sent out search parties, but they couldn't find him. He had the guards questioned, but they didn't have any answers. "All right," said Herod. "Then we'll just have those guards killed." ■

Acts 12:1-19

A Dream

Good old Peter.
He thought it was just a dream.
He couldn't believe
You would really send an angel for him,
Father.
Well, I probably wouldn't believe it
either.
Maybe Peter thought he wasn't important
enough
for You to care that much.
I feel that way about myself sometimes too.
But the truth is that You *did* send that
angel.
And You do care for me too.
You thought Peter was that important
and You think I am too.
You take both of us very seriously
—and that's no dream.
So maybe I'd better start
taking myself a little more seriously too!

Paul the Missionary

One day the Holy Spirit told Saul—whose name had been changed to Paul—and a man called Barnabas to set out on some travels and tell people in distant lands about Jesus.

So first they went to Seleucia and from there they sailed to Cyprus. They landed at a place called Salamis and began to teach about Jesus in the synagogs there.

Paul and Barnabas traveled the whole length of the island and at a place called Paphos they met a magician called Bar-jesus. This magician worked for a Roman official called Sergius, who was a very intelligent man.

Sergius sent for Paul and Barnabas because he wanted to hear about Jesus. But the magician didn't like that idea at all.

Finally Paul looked him right in the eye. "You are an impostor!" he said. "You are a cheat, a son of the devil, and an enemy of all true religion. Why don't you stop twisting God's ways? You just watch now how God's hand is going to strike you. For a while now you are going to be blind."

At that very minute, everything got misty for the magician. He groped around and had to find someone to lead him. Meanwhile, Sergius, who had watched the whole thing, was astonished and began to believe in Jesus at once.

Paul and Barnabas traveled to many other places too and one day they came to the countryside around the towns of Lystra and Derbe. There they met a man who had been crippled ever since he had been born. This man listened to Paul's preaching.

Paul could tell that the man had faith, so he said, "Get up on your feet. Stand up!"

The crippled man jumped up and began to walk.

When the people in the crowd saw this, they got a crazy idea.

"These men are gods!" they cried, pointing to Paul and Barnabas. "They have come to us disguised as men!" They began calling Barnabas Zeus and Paul Hermes. Then the priests brought oxen and flowers to Paul and Barnabas. They wanted to make a sacrifice to the men they thought were gods.

When Paul and Barnabas realized what was happening, they tore their clothes and began to shout. "Friends!" they yelled. "We are only people like you! We have come with the Good News of Jesus so you will stop worshiping idols."

The people didn't sacrifice the oxen after that, but they still didn't really believe Paul and Barnabas. Then some other people came along and turned the crowd against the two missionaries. They began to stone Paul and finally they dragged him outside the town and left him. They thought he was dead.

Some of Jesus' followers hurried after them and gathered around Paul. But they had no sooner got there, when Paul stood up and marched right back into the town. He still had a lot of work to do! ■

Acts 13:4-12; 14:8-20

Prayer

No cars, no trains, no jets.
Poor Paul had to travel on foot
or on a donkey or a leaky ship.
But he went, Father.
I think he was so excited about Jesus
that he couldn't help telling the world.
I won't have as much trouble as Paul.
All I have to worry about is feeling shy
or embarrassed
or a little scared.
Fill me with some of Paul's excitement,
Father,
so I just can't help telling the world.
Amen.

Paul in Philippi

After a while, Paul began traveling with a man called Silas. Then a young man called Timothy joined them.

One night Paul had a dream. In the dream he saw a man from Macedonia calling to him.

"Come to Macedonia and help us," said the man. At once Paul got ready to go to Macedonia. Finally he got to Philippi, the main city in one part of Macedonia. He stayed for a few days and then he went out to the river to pray.

There he met a group of women who believed in God and began to preach to them. One of them was called Lydia. She sold purple dye and was a good woman. After she heard what Paul had to say about Jesus, Lydia and everyone in her house were baptized. Then she insisted that Paul come and stay with them.

One day as Paul and Silas were on their way to pray, they met a slave girl who worked as a soothsayer. She told fortunes and made a lot of money for her owners that way. This girl began to follow Paul and shouted, "Here are the servants of the Most High! They are going to tell you how to be saved!"

She did this for several days and finally Paul lost his temper.

He turned to the girl and said to the evil spirit inside her, "In the name of Jesus I order you to leave this girl."

At once the spirit left. Now this meant that the girl wasn't able to tell fortunes anymore and that made her owners mad. They grabbed Paul and Silas and took them to court.

"These men are causing trouble in the city!" they said angrily. The crowds in the court began shouting against Paul and Silas too, so the judges had them beaten and thrown into prison.

"Keep a close watch on these two," they ordered the jailer.

So the jailer put them in the inside cell and fastened their feet in wooden stocks.

Paul and Silas didn't seem too bothered by all this, though. Late that night they sat in their cell, praying and singing praises to God.

Suddenly there was an earthquake and the whole prison shook and trembled. The doors to all the cells flew open and the chains fell off the prisoners.

The jailer woke up and saw the open doors. His first thought was that all his prisoners had escaped. At once he grabbed his sword. He thought he might as well kill himself before his bosses killed him instead.

"Stop!" shouted Paul. "Don't hurt yourself. All of your prisoners are here."

The jailer asked for the lights to be lit. Then he ran into Paul and Silas' cell and threw himself at their feet.

"Here, come out with me," he said. "You are free. But tell me, what must I do to be saved?"

"Believe in Jesus," said Paul and Silas. Then they told the jailer and everyone in his house about Jesus. The jailer washed Paul and Silas' wounds and then he and all his household were baptized. Then he fed them a meal and the whole family celebrated because they knew about Jesus now.

The next morning a message came from the judges. "Let Paul and Silas go," it said.

"You can go now," said the jailer. "The judges said so."

"They did, did they?" said Paul. "Well, they've made one mistake. They didn't know when they beat us and threw us into prison that we are Roman citizens. It's illegal for them to do things like that to Roman citizens. Now they can just come themselves and escort us out of town."

When the judges found out that Paul and Silas really were Roman citizens, they were horrified at what they had done. They came to the prison and politely begged Paul and Silas to leave town.

Paul and Silas went to Lydia's house first, though. They saw everyone and talked to them a little more. Then they left town. ■

Acts 16:9-40

Out of This World

That Paul acted like
he was out of this world, Father.
He didn't do any of the things
ordinary people would do.
He didn't get scared when they sent him
to prison.
He sat there and prayed and sang
songs instead.
He didn't escape when he had the chance.
Instead he tried to keep the jailer
out of trouble.
And what happened?
His prayers were answered.
The jailer and his family believed in Jesus.
And the judges apologized.
Paul was out of this world all right.
He was in Your world,
Your kingdom.
And things just work differently there!

Paul Goes to Rome

Paul traveled to many places, told many people about Jesus, and started many churches. He wrote letters to his churches too. In these letters he reminded them of the Good News about Jesus. He helped them solve their problems and he told them to be brave.

At last, though, Paul was arrested and finally the officials decided to send him to Rome. He and some of Jesus' other followers got on a ship with Roman soldiers and set sail. But the winds were against them and traveling was difficult.

One day Paul said, "This is going to be dangerous. We might not only lose the cargo and the ship. We might lose our lives as well."

The soldiers didn't pay any attention to this warning, and once again the ship set sail.

Soon a hurricane came rushing toward them and drove the ship ahead of it. Finally the soldiers had to throw the cargo overboard. Then they threw the ship's gear after it. Still the storm raged and after several days everyone was sure they would all be killed.

Then Paul stood up and said, "Friends, if you had listened to me, none of this would have happened. But now I tell you not to worry. No one will be killed. Last night God sent an angel to me. He told me not to be afraid. He said that I would get to Rome and, because of me, all of you would be safe too. So trust in God. We will be cast ashore on some island."

On the morning of the 14th day, Paul encouraged everyone to eat something. "You will not die," he promised them.

So the people ate and that very day their ship ran aground on the island of Malta.

Some of the soldiers wanted to kill the prisoners so they wouldn't escape. But the officer guarding Paul wouldn't let them do that.

The people who lived on the island were very kind to the people from the ship. They built a huge fire for them because it was cold and rain had begun to fall.

Paul was helping to collect firewood too when all at once a snake crawled out of the wood and grabbed his hand.

When the people from the island saw this, they thought Paul was really a terrible criminal and that God was going to kill him. But Paul just shook the snake into the fire and went on about his business. When the island people saw that he wasn't going to die, they decided that maybe he was a god instead.

A government official named Publius lived on the island and he invited Paul and his friends to stay with him. Publius' father was in the house too and he was very sick. Paul went in to see him, prayed, laid his hands on him, and made him well again. The other island people heard about this and began bringing more sick people to Paul. By the time the ship was ready to sail again, the island people had loaded it up with all sorts of food so the people on it could have a more comfortable journey.

At last the ship sailed on and finally they came to Rome. There Paul talked to the Jewish people and explained how he had been arrested.

"The Romans aren't mad at me," he said. "It's the Jewish people in Jerusalem that are."

"You must tell us all about it then," said the Jewish people in Rome. So Paul spent a whole day with them and told them about Jesus. Some of them began to believe in Him, but others didn't.

Paul stayed in Rome for two years. He lived in a house that he rented and many people came to visit him. Paul told all of them about God's kingdom and about Jesus and no one tried to stop him. ∎

Acts 27—28

Prayer

Paul wrote about many things
in his letters to the churches.
I don't really understand a lot of them.
But I understand
the most important thing, Father,
because Paul says it again and again.
You loved us so much
that You sent Your Son
to die for us and rise again.
And now we are Yours forever.
Alleluia, Father! Alleluia!

Amen.

My Favorite Songs

Thy Loving-Kindness

Text: *Traditional*
Tune: *Loving-kindness*
Setting: *Charles Ore (1936—   )*

How Precious Is the Book Divine

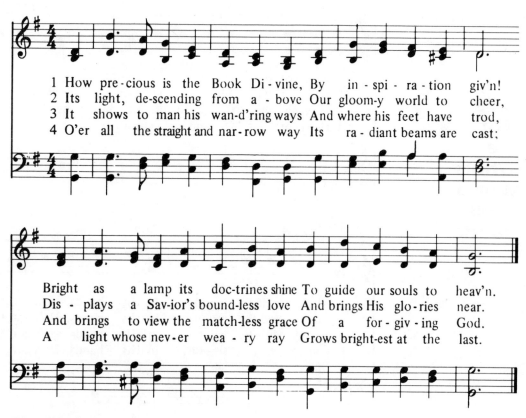

1 How pre-cious is the Book Di-vine, By in-spi-ra-tion giv'n!
2 Its light, de-scending from a-bove Our gloom-y world to cheer,
3 It shows to man his wan-d'ring ways And where his feet have trod,
4 O'er all the straight and nar-row way Its ra-diant beams are cast;

Bright as a lamp its doc-trines shine To guide our souls to heav'n.
Dis-plays a Sav-ior's bound-less love And brings His glo-ries near.
And brings to view the match-less grace Of a for-giv-ing God.
A light whose nev-er wea-ry ray Grows bright-est at the last.

Text: *John Fawcett (1749—1817)*
Tune: **Walder**, *Johann Jakob Walder (1750—1817)*

**He's
Got
the
Whole
World
in His
Hands**

1 He's got the whole world in His hands, He's got the
2 He's got the wind and the rain in His hands, He's got the
3 He's got the ti-ny lit-tle ba-by in His hands, He's got the
4 He's got you and me, broth-er, in His hands, He's got

whole wide world in His hands, He's got the whole
sun and the moon in His hands, He's got the wind and the
ti-ny lit-tle ba-by in His hands, He's got the ti-ny lit-tle
you and me, sis-ter, in His hands, He's got you and me,

world in His hands, He's got the whole world in His hands.
rain in His hands, He's got the whole world in His hands.
ba-by in His hands, He's got the whole world in His hands.
broth-er, in His hands, He's got the whole world in His hands.

Text: American spiritual
*Tune: **In His hands** (American spiritual)*

From *Joyful Sounds.* Setting © 1977 Concordia Publishing House. Used by permission.

My Faith Looks Up to Thee

1 My faith looks up to Thee, Thou Lamb of Cal - va - ry,
2 May Thy rich grace im - part Strength to my faint - ing heart,

Sav - ior di - vine. Now hear me while I pray; Take all my
My zeal in - spire! As Thou hast died for me, Oh, may my

guilt a - way; Oh, let me from this day Be whol - ly Thine!
love to Thee Pure, warm, and changeless be, A liv - ing fire! A - men.

Text: Ray Palmer (1808—87), cento
*Tune: **Olivet**, Lowell Mason (1792—1872)*

Prayer of Thanks

Father, You made this world
and all the people in it.
But You didn't go away
when You were finished.
You stayed with us
and got mixed up in our lives.
It was was wonderful, Father.
And then
You had people write it down,
the whole story of what happened—
of how You brought Your people out of Egypt,
of how You sent Your Son to set us free,
of how You made us into a church.
It's all there, Father—
the story of Your love,
the story of Your people,
our story.
Thank You!

Amen.